Plants Are Terrible People

Plants Are Terrible People

Luke Ruggenberg

For Penstemon

III/V

This garden isn't the same without you

Table of Contents

Welcome

ait wait wait! No, hang on, it's not ready yet—
I mean <*ahem*> please ... do come in.

Welcome to my garden, friends. Everything is entirely as it should be, and I am completely prepared for your visit. The beds are weeded and watered. Mostly. The grass is ... cut? We'll say the grass is cut. The children's toys have been made less of an *immediate* tripping hazard. The plants are ... in their proper place. Well, they're in the ground, anyway. And why would it be otherwise? RIGHT?! *HAHAHA*! Ha ...

Sorry. Uh, well, please enjoy some snacks. I hope you like juice boxes and string cheese. What can I say? The kids helped me with the shopping. Oh! But there is some wine over there. If I were you, I would avail yourselves thereof; you're going to need it.

If you happen to encounter anything … unusual during your tour, please pay no mind. You're probably just seeing things. There's nothing strange about my garden.

Nothing.

Or else everything is strange; I can't remember, it's one of the two.

I'll tell you what, you go on ahead and look around. Take your time, enjoy your visit, there's no … imminent danger. I mean, it wouldn't hurt to bring your hori-hori knife, you know, *just* in case. But no, feel free to take some notes, get your picture taken, *signthiswaiver*—ask a few questions, and then we'll all meet up back here, so you can all … well, so you can all leave.

…

What? No. Ha! I didn't say "waiver." I said, "mind the pavers." They're, uh, the paving stones are a little uneven so … watch your step? Ha! Waiver—why would you need to sign a waiver to visit a garden? Preposterous. There's nothing safer and more predictable than a *garden*, right?

Right?

Fellow Weeds

I'd like to start off with a thought experiment, if I may. Who's ready for a thought experiment? Anyone? Well, too bad, because this one is already whistling down on you like a bomb from one of those seminally violent old Saturday morning cartoons. Best skedaddle if you want out. No hard feelings, just throw the book against the wall and run out of the room screaming right now. Although I'm not sure what you're so afraid of—it's not as if those cartoon bombs ever actually hurt anyone. They just gave us a good laugh and taught us about unilateral conflict escalation. So chill.

Thank you. Now, part one of my thought experiment is—

...

Sorry, *yes*, there's more than one part.

...

Well, yes, you can still run out of the room screaming, if you must, but this is ridiculous. I shouldn't have to sit here and spell out how to avoid my thought experiment. It's meant to be fun. If you can't handle fun, then let the words pass through you, meaningless, as you read them, your mind resonant with the sweet *om* of nothingness. Empty. Like you're watching TV. Jeez. Or skip ahead to the next chapter. May I continue?

Okay, so my (apparently much-dreaded) question for you, fellow plant people, is this:

If you could choose any plant in the world, what kind would you be?

There now! That wasn't so bad, was it?

If I know gardeners, I would be willing to bet a generous shovelful of you have already considered this very question at some point in the past. It's one of those random, effervescent what-ifs, which like to bubble up through the froth and stick in your head during a prolonged weeding session, often accompanied by such timeless gardening mysteries as, *where did I set my damned pruners?* and, *why am I doing this, again?* If this is you, then you've got a head start. Others who, like me, have kids of a certain age, and have thus forevermore sacrificed such idle thinking to the *Moana* film soundtrack blasting in perpetuity through their skulls, may need a moment to catch up. If you do find yourself in the latter group, then this is your chance; it's grown up time! Quick now, before you can recall the name of Moana's pet chicken—what kind of plant would you be? If you could strut the stem and lace up the roots of any plant in the world, which would you choose? Out of the whole wide sweep of leafy things, where do you fit in?

I know, it's not easy. There is so much to consider. What kind of buds would you boast? Which foliage would you flaunt? Something wild and untamed, or clipped and prim? How do you feel about lignin? Photosynthetic pathways? Should you take the plunge and go with zygomorphic flowers, or stick with actinomorphic? Should you maybe learn what those mean? And let's talk cotyledons: do you fancy yourself mono- or di-?

...

Sorry—I've been informed by HR that my last question may have crossed a line. For the record, let it be known that

I support all cotyledon orientations equally, and in no way did I mean to offend or provoke anyone. My sincere apologies, it's hard to tell what passes for taboo when talking to plants. All I can say is, they're surprisingly prudish for a bunch that's keen on wagging their reproductive parts out in the open air. Nevertheless, to avoid trouble, I shall henceforth adhere to a strictly "Your seed-leaf, your business" policy and hope the matter blows over.

Let's try a different approach to the question. Don't you remember, as kids, trying to come up with the most awesome superpower for your make-believe alter-ego? Flying, telekinesis, exploding karate kicks, that sort of stuff? Well this is the same thing, only way cooler. At least for the admittedly thin slice of the demographic pie who might have picked up this volume in the first place. The rest of you can duke it out over superstrength vs. atomic sneezes or lightening-charged jazz hands; us gardeners will vigorously debate the merits of tubers vs. corms.

(For the record: I say tubers. Definitely tubers. But why not *atomic* tubers?)

Your time is up, anyway. Have you decided yet? What kind of plant would you be? Perennial? Annual? Tree? Shrub?

One of those creepy chlorophyll-lacking parasitic plants? A fern maybe? Any cycads out there? They've been around since the dinosaurs, you know.

In coming to a decision do you choose the plant that you, as a human, find the most alluring, hoping that in your transmogrified state you will be assured a lifetime of fawning admiration? Or, do you address any latent insecurities you may have about the frailties of your animal body by slapping on some plant-style reinforcements? I'm talking thorns, toxins, thick bark, immortal meristem systems like grasses have so you can regrow after being chopped down or munched on. Choose your weapon. Did you know that yew trees produce a chemical that can fight off cancer? And they can live for a thousand years. Also, one assumes they are far less likely to be involved in motorcycle accidents. Yews might be onto something. And *you* might be onto something, you *yew* you.

Perhaps this chance for personal rebranding titillates your wild side. Is that you all tingly-eager to thrust your frilly petal parts into the spring orgy of drunken bees and hummingbirds?

. . .

(Sorry, that'll be HR again. Another line crossed. Point taken, apologies, moving on.)

Or, rather than indulge, would you play the obnoxious, selfless martyr, even here, in an anonymous thought experiment? You know who you are. *I would be wheat so I could feed the world.* BS you'd be wheat. And let me guess, your superpower would be hugs. Wheat hugs. You'd be an ever-hugging stalk of wheat, with gluten intolerance as your kryptonite. Well, that and HR complaints. Take it from me, those guys aren't letting anything slide; not everyone wants to be hugged, all right, wheat bread?

Whichever factors influence your decision, it's best not to overthink this part of the experiment. Just trust your gut and choose something cool so we can move on. How about a rhododendron? Simple enough. Pretty flowers, evergreen, nothing too crazy, everyone's happy. It's settled: you'd be a rhododendron. Watch out for root weevils.

Now, for part two of the experiment. (There's only *two* parts, settle down.) Once you've decided on a blue-sky, follow-your-dreams, there's-no-wrong-answer-besides-wheat, response to part one, it's time to get real. Forget about what you want to be. What kind of plant are you, *really*?

Allow me to express regret to those of you who managed to scrape just enough rust off the old imagination to soar briefly in the warm breeze of *what-if,* only for this cruel follow-up to strike you from the sky. But it is critical to the soul of the experiment. So once you've climbed from your twisted wreckage of barely lofted dreams, and breathed a heavy earthbound sigh, do give it some thought. I'll wait.

Sorry, you've still got a little bit of burning dream on you—right there. Kind of all over. Remember: stop, drop, and roll …

There you go, that's better.

Now, be honest. There's nothing to be gained from self-deception. Look at yourself hard in that mirror. What's looking back at you? Which plant accurately reflects your own unique combination of traits; physical, psychological, spiritual—

…

No, no, you're not being *honest.* Oh, for the love of—stop saying you're *wheat!* You're not WHEAT, okay?! Can you get that through your skull? What mirror are you even looking at?

No, you know what? Forget it. I will not be derailed by you, Wheatabix. I will soldier forth for the sake of those readers more inclined to take their casual, horticultural suppositions with due gravity and respect. We're trying to learn something about ourselves and you're out there threshing yourself in a delusion of cereal grandeur.

Now, may I continue?

Look, I'll go first if it will help. Here's the author taking one for the team.

What plant am I?

Well, after some careful consideration and soul-searching, it seems clear that I am ... that is to say, the plant that most precisely captures my own personality, my strengths, and weaknesses has to be, uh ...

Well, shoot, this *is* harder than it sounds. And not nearly as much fun as choosing which plant you *want* to be. Can I go back to that question for a minute? Because I'd be a giant red cedar tree if I could. They're just awesome. Towering above the forest, rot resistant, wonderful smell, shaggy, peeling bark with lots of uses—did you know they live so long they're almost guaranteed to be struck by lightning at some point in their life? It's true. Old-growth forests in the

Pacific Northwest have lots of these gargantuan, ancient red cedars with dead, lightening-scorched leaders. It looks devastating, when you see one. But the amazing thing is, once struck, the tree isn't destroyed, it just shoots up a new leader out to one side and goes on living for a few hundred more years! For the rest of its life, it bears the ghastly scar of that one blinding flash that shivered a million degrees down its spine and would have killed anything else on Earth. But it, the red cedar, carries on, a stalwart monument to grace and perseverance in the face of unthinkable violence.

That would be neat, right?

But unfortunately, I'm *not* a cedar tree now, am I? As much as I'd like to be able to claim that enormous cache of symbolic strength and resilience, it's not the plant that best represents me. Only time will tell how I'll weather the storms that strike me, the scars I'll carry, and which phantom pains will linger on. Maybe in time my own gray leader will speak of the pain I've endured, the tragedies through which I've prevailed. But regardless, and in the meantime, I am, at the very least, *much* shorter than a cedar tree. It's all wrong. A squat, stumpy red cedar would I be.

So, maybe a shorter plant is the key. And one whose success is measured not by towering achievements or ancient strength, but by its ability to kick around underfoot and hang in there. A plant that takes each day as it comes and tries hard to catch the rays of life's fleeting fortunes, all while not being too terribly eaten or stomped upon.

The more I think about it … the more I must admit I am, probably, just some sort of a weed.

Ouch.

Yes, a weed, and a common one at that. It doesn't especially matter which kind. Maybe it has a name, a specific epithet, but only a niche botanist would bother learning it. You yourself might acknowledge it if it were growing in your garden, but only if it proved to be enough of a nuisance to demand attention from your hoe. Or if it got into your strawberries. Otherwise—meh, it's no big deal.

Now, lest you think all this weedy, woe-is-me talk is just rote self-deprecation, allow me to suggest that you too— whoever you are—might also be a weed. Woe is *you*. Sorry. There are a lot of weeds in the world. And in the slapdash Venn-diagram of quack psychology and plant ecology we've sketched out here today, it turns out that most of us are, by one circle or another, weeds.

...

No, not *wheat*—weeds, *weeds* you insufferable—

Nope. Huh-uh. Never mind. I'm just going to ignore it. Doctor says I can't get so worked up about troublesome, imaginary readers. Blood pressure and all that. Deep breaths, and *1 ... 2 ... 3 ...*

Now, I know you all were hoping for something a *little* more interesting or endearing as your spirit plant, but the honest truth is that weeds are everywhere. As gardeners, we ought to know that better than anyone.

Still, there is redemption to be had here, in identifying with weeds. But, since our view of these plants is from across untold generations of territorial battle lines, we are not particularly inclined to feel any affinity towards their kind. Perhaps a grudging respect for their tenacity occasionally crosses the mind, but nothing likely to spawn admiration or aspiration in the realm of contrived, trans-species identification, which is, after all, what we're looking for here.

But if you could stand back for a moment, and see them dispassionately, armed with an open mind instead of a stirrup-hoe, you'd be forced to acknowledge this one simple fact about weeds: they are really, *really* good at being weeds. And when you think about it, that makes them really, *really* good at being plants. Which is what they're meant to be, and really all that matters in this free-for-all brawl of life—being what you are, with conviction and competence, and in frank repudiation of any Gardener On High who thinks he gets to decide who goes where.

Are weeds going to win any ribbons at the state fair by boasting the biggest, gaudiest blooms? No. But on the plus side, no one's cutting their heads off to display at a state fair. Do they have the most saccharin, cloying fruits as determined by us, the hooting apes with silly hats? Again, no. But that means they're far less likely to be eaten by said apes. Another win. Above all, do they adapt to the whims and wiles of the universe well enough to keep coming back, with grace and ferocity, season after season, to do what they do until they can't anymore? You better believe they do.

In fact, I think I might be proud to call myself a weed. Leave the garden to those divas more concerned with appearance, place, and praise. Let them falter when the gardener turns his back. Let them wilt in the fickle blinding glare of fashion. I'll be growing in the cracks, grabbing hold of the earth with everything I've got, because that's what I'm good at.

And you're welcome to join me.

The way I see it, you can either spend your life pretending to be something you're not, in the hope that deception will earn you a spot in bed next to the roses and dahlias and other floral fancypants; or, you can sprout right where you are. Take root like you mean it. Laugh and grit your teeth and cast your seed and bloom your bloom because *you* know it's beautiful. That slash of sunlight you worked so hard to reach will be all the sweeter because you earned it. You choked back the poisons sprayed down on you; you dodged the spades and blades bent on turning you under. You grew stronger through it all. You are indomitable, a glorious nuisance to all those pampered pretties lashed to stakes and dreading leaf spot in the garden around you. You are here, and you are you, and you aren't going anywhere just yet. If that makes you a weed in some snobby gardener's eye, so be it. To your fellow weeds—and there are a lot of us—you are nothing short of a superhero.

<u>Missing!</u>

<u>Hori-Hori Knife</u>

Don't worry about what it's called—it's a Japanese
weeding tool that resembles a wicked hunting knife.
About eight inches long, has a wooden handle with a
piece of bright orange tape wrapped around it, which is
supposed to help me not lose it.

Needless to say, the tape didn't work.

Last seen right here in my stupid hand. I think. Unless …
wait a minute—I didn't see my *son* wandering around
with it, did I?

Hold on—where's my son?!

<u>Also Missing!</u>

Toddler boy gone rogue! Possibly wielding what looks to
be an orange-handled hunting knife.

If found, return both promptly, and please forget this ever
happened.

A Reckoning

knock on the door. How long since that sound
had meant anything good? How many decades of
pranks, solicitations, and porch-borne bad news
had sullied the once neighborly act of visitation? Somewhere
along the way, the rap of knuckles on wood had lost the
benefit of the doubt. No one's heart leapt at the sound
anymore. Not in the right direction, anyway.

Larry's house even had a doorbell, so when the knock
reverberated like a migraine through the walls, it was even
more dreadful in its apparent disdain for the more cheerful
alternative. This was melody passed over for percussion; this
was violence in lieu of song. Larry's home was being punched
in the face.

He heard it all the way from the back yard. Hose wand in hand, he had been watering the potted herbs. Again. They wilted so quickly this time of year. When the knock came, a chill flooded through him despite the afternoon heat. For a moment, startled, he thought the distraction at the door had caused him to accidentally douse himself in cold water. But no, his blood simply knew what the knock meant before his brain did. His heart sluiced ice. He shuddered.

The time for reckoning had come.

"Honey?" he called weakly, knowing full well his wife would be at work still. He was alone and he would face this alone. As it should be. It was his heavy hand at the spigot all summer long, his thumb on the ergonomic, carpal-tunnel-friendly, watering wand trigger, not hers. It was Larry who set their bedside alarm to "reveille" in the pre-dawn gloom of summer days, so that he could shuffle outside and open the floodgates, not his wife. Hers was the voice of reason and temperance, a voice he rarely heard over the chattering of sprinklers and cursing at kinked hoses which became his own voice as the days in the garden grew long and parched. He alone would march up to that booming door and face the consequences of his actions.

Or—another thought—he could jump over the neighbor's fence and flee the country. Just until things settled down, or until he could figure out how to fake his own death. Shave his hair off, get a new ID, start life over as a man named Warren or Jake or—

But no. No. He could do this.

He took a few deep breaths to steel himself for the showdown. A few more and he was just hyperventilating. Larry couldn't remember how breathing worked. He wobbled on spongy knees back through the house. He became vaguely aware, as he went, that he was dragging the hose through the living room, but he refused to let go of the solid, comforting grip the wand provided. As a weapon of choice, it lacked a certain oomph, but as an object around which his shaking hand could steady itself, it was first-rate. So, there was that.

He barely registered the hose catching on a side table and knocking over the handsome antique lamp his wife had fallen in love with during their trip to New York. This was a lamp which had proven so costly to ship back home that they had sacrificed two nights of their stay in order to recoup the cost. It was a good lamp, and she loved it. In time, Larry had come to love it too. Now it was on the floor, in pieces. This was a good reason not to drag hoses through the house. There are many.

When he reached the entryway, Larry couldn't open the door. Standing there, hose in hand, mouth open slightly, he absorbed the heavy knocks as they came, recoiling slightly with each blow like a sorry punching bag. His heart fluttered with the arrhythmic beat on the door. There came a glimmer of perverse hope with the sensation. Some sort of diversionary heart attack would, at this moment, be less unwelcome than usual, a cardiac equivalent of "saved by the bell." But alas, his heart thumped indignantly along, refusing to play scapegoat to what was, after all, a weakness of the spirit and not the flesh.

Larry absently wondered, as he stood there not opening the door, what percentage of his local taxes secretly went toward funding shadowy enforcement arms of public utilities; for example, of the sort that might be sent out into peaceful neighborhoods to batter doors and exact penance from delinquent citizens. It suddenly seemed obvious, in his paranoia, that such agencies would exist, and that agents of such agencies had been covertly staking out his home for months now. He further wondered, hypothetically, how much these agents might be paid, and whether they might accept bribes in exchange for not knocking on his door anymore. Also, hypothetically, could he, Larry, afford to pay such a bribe? Hypothetically, would he?

Who was he kidding, they were probably highly specialized contract workers. No way could he afford that level of corruption.

"Larry Smith?!"

The voice startled him, and he let out a yelp. So much for being a good, dumb punching bag. He froze and hoped with renewed zeal that the man at the door would leave. He hoped harder than he had hoped since childhood, with the results one came to expect as an adult.

"Sir?" it was a deep, gruff voice. The cliché of it annoyed him. He imagined, behind the door, every goon, enforcer, and hit man he'd ever seen on TV. It was overkill. "Sir, I know you're there, I heard you."

So, he had racked up a big water bill trying to keep his garden alive during the summer. There was no need to send hired muscle to break down his door. Was there? And would they? Just how big *was* his water bill? He'd been scared to look at, or even open it last month because it seemed quite a bit, well … thicker than a utility bill should be. Which shouldn't be thick at all, really.

"Hello? Come on, sir. I think you know why I'm here."

Then there were the daily phone calls from an unrecognized local number, which he refused to answer. And the voicemails he "forgot" to check daily. And the unusually large team of meter-readers that spilled forth from a city-marked panel van like clowns from their funny little car to double-check his meter. Was it functioning properly? Was it perhaps possessed by demons, or in close proximity to a localized and especially chaotic rift in space-time? He had ignored the issue as aggressively as he knew how, and still it wouldn't go away.

"I'm sorry, sir, could you at least turn off the sprinkler that's hitting the porch here? I'm getting soaked."

"Dahlias!" Larry shouted, whether in defense, or explanation, or out of a simple need to say something, anything, was unclear.

"What?!" the gruff voice called back through the door, incredulous.

"The sprinkler! The dahlias! They're … they're *dry!*"

"It's ... it's summer, sir, everything's dry—I'm sorry, could you just open the door, so we don't have to shout at each other?"

"Who's shouting?!" Larry shouted.

"Sir, please, we've been trying to get a hold of you for a couple weeks now. I'm with the city water department and, uh, well, we just wanted to make sure that you weren't turning your property into some kind of aquarium or ... illegal water park or, like, maybe you accidentally left all your sinks running while you went on vacation for two months, or ... well, I, personally just wanted to see if maybe your house was literally under a few feet of water. We've kind of got an office pool going. Could be a broken pipe somewhere, I guess, too ... although I'm now seeing a, uh, well, a lot of hoses and sprinklers in your garden. Wow, like, a *lot*. Nice garden, though. What are those bushes over there? Some kind of blueberries?"

Larry finally opened the door.

"They're bl-black currants ... actually," he said to the dripping man on the porch, whose swarthy bulk came as no surprise. "Now w-why don't you tell me why you're really here?" He meant it to sound tough, or angry, or maybe nonchalant, but since he hadn't decided ahead of time, and since his voice shook with the same tremor as his hands, which caused him to reflexively clench his jaw halfway through the question, it didn't sound like any of those things. It sounded like an unwell recluse with a nerve condition trying not to vomit.

"Sorry, what's that?" the big man asked. He looked as if beneath his tight, white polo shirt and slacks he was stacked up from cast-off bricks and concrete. "I don't understand. Are you feeling okay, sir? Why are you dragging a hose through the house?"

"This … this isn't a hose," Larry attempted lamely, then gave up. "What are you going to do? Slash my tires, cut off a finger, spread salt on my garden? Whatever it is, just get it over with, before my wife gets home, you sonofa—!"

"Whoa—no, sir, I told you, I'm from the city. Water. My name's Alonso. They sent me out to make sure everything's okay. This property's been, uh, using a lot of water. Sooo much water."

"I HAVE RAIN BARRELS!" Larry said, way too loudly. He was having a hard time regulating his voice.

"Huh?"

"Rain barrels. But they've been empty for a month." Now he was whispering. The two extremes did not average out to anything like normal.

"That's … admirable, sir. Maybe you could—"

"Drought tolerant!"

"Huh?"

"I … uh, I plant drought-tolerant plants whenever I can but, you know, even drought-tolerant plants, you have to water to get them established for a year or two, or five, and then of course it's hard to have a veggie garden that's drought-tolerant, so I gotta water that, and berries and herbs and fruit trees need water, and all the pots, and that one bed that's under the big maple tree that always gets dry no matter what you plant there! I'm just trying to get stuff established, you know, but eventually, eventually, I mean this stuff shouldn't need so much water, and by then I'll have a couple more rain barrels and—"

"Sir, whoa! Please."

"I. Use. SOAKER HOSES!"

" … "

"Mostly. And I water in the morning or evening."

"Uh … it's two in the afternoo— "

"MOSTLY!" Larry's breath came ragged. He was sweating.

"I'm not … threatening you." Alonso put on a good show of not threatening Larry, holding his meaty hands palms out. "I mean, you're the one who's going to have to pay your water bill when it's due, but—"

"Or what?! Look, I swear I'll cut back! I'll—I'll stop watering *everything*, only the bare minimum, only the necessities! I'll—"

"Sir, uh, even as we speak, you're using that hose you dragged through the house to water this here big pot on the porch that is also, I hate to say, well within the range of two separate sprinklers that are running."

"I … I am? Well, yes, like I said, only the necessities. This is a … very important pot." Larry couldn't seem to turn the hose off.

"There's … there's nothing *in* the pot, sir. It's just dirt." The hit man's—or whoever he was—head had been tilting ever so slightly throughout their conversation, as though some undiscovered, obtuse angle of view might snap Larry's crooked, sodden world into focus.

"*Soil,*" Larry mewed. "I'm prepping the *soil.* There's nothing planted yet, but as soon as I find the right variety of Japanese white pine—it's very rare, I can show you pictures—I'm going to put it here, and it's good to water the *soil* ahead of time. Makes for an easier transition for the tree."

"So, you're watering a tree … that you don't have yet?" The hose had long since filled the pot beyond the saturation point of the soil and water now flowed freely over the rim. "Sir … why don't you, uh, why don't you just hand me the hose?" Alonso seemed concerned, but Larry had no doubt that was part of the act.

"Wh-what hose, what are you talking about?"

"The one in your hands."

"Sorry, I don't know what you—YOU'LL HAVE TO CATCH ME FIRST!" Larry turned suddenly and sprinted back through the house, knocking over two more lamps on his way to the backyard. It suddenly seemed like they had a lot of lamps.

"Please don't run!" Alonso called. "This is undignified, and you don't look to be in running shape! I asked for the hose, not your life!"

"THEY ARE <pantpant> ONE AND THE SAME! <Gasp> IF MY GARDEN WILTS, SO DO I! COME GET ME YOU BASTARD!"

"Umm. No thank you, Sir!" Alonso stepped gingerly through Larry's house, righting several overturned lamps along the way. He kept both hands in plain sight as he stepped through the patio door and into the fenced backyard where Larry was dashing back and forth like a trapped animal. A continuous shower issued from the watering wand, which he twirled overhead as he frantically tried to douse everything in the garden one last time. This was a surprisingly difficult action to coordinate while running, so Larry kept reversing motion, running backwards, and tripping as the hose wound around his legs.

Alonso shook his head in pity.

"Gardeners," he muttered under his breath. "Uh, sir?" he called as he traced the hose back to a spigot near the corner of the house. "I'm going to … I'm going to do something here. I just wanna help, trust me!"

Larry's last fall had left him sprawled out on the lawn, seemingly for good. At some point during his desperate, helicoptering irrigation attempt, he had subconsciously engaged the trigger lock for the hose wand, which now lay at his side, spraying a constant stream of water into his gasping, spluttering face. Larry wondered if anyone had ever drowned while watering a garden.

Alonso, having reached the spigot, called out one last warning.

"Okay, sir! You may never have explored this function of your outdoor plumbing, so please don't freak out! I mean, more than you already are! Seems unlikely that's possible, so here goes!" And with that, he turned the spigot *clockwise*, recruiting a valve that had gone unused since time in the garden began.

As the hose stream slowed to an exhausted dribble, Larry gasped. The silence! The absence! No more hiss of spray and clack of sprinklers. No more guttural groan of water rushing through unseen pipes. No more calculations grinding in his head to estimate the penetration of water into the various soils and subsoils of the yard.

Birds were chirping! Neighborhood kids—playing! And was that an ice cream truck driving by? It was all too much. His sweat and tears soaked into the ground with the last of the hose's lifeblood. He felt months and years of angst seep into the earth and disappear.

"Thank you … Alonso!" he whispered in his savior's direction, choking back the tears. Alonso just shook his head.

"Yeah, no problem," he said. "Believe it or not, sir, it's not the first time I've had to do this. I'll tell Angie at the office that she won the pool this time. Easy money, I shoulda guessed 'gardener.' Ah well, maybe next time." As he passed by Larry, he dropped a hefty envelope onto his soggy torso with a splat. "Just remember to pay your bill, sir. $3800 is a pretty good one," he chuckled. "Goodbye now!"

Underfoot, Larry could only groan as tears once more filled his eyes.

Recipes From My Garden

Roasted Winter Squash

Preparation Time: 1-5 years

Cook Time: 1 hour

This one is a favorite. There is nothing like the subtle sweetness and simplicity of rich, warm squash in the drear of winter. It took me a few tries to get this recipe right, and it may for you as well. Step #3 is a doozy, and many folks seem to get hung up there. But is it worth all the time and effort when you finally bite into that delicious squash? In hindsight, no, probably not.

1) Preheat oven to 400°F.

2) Fill baking dish with ½ inch of water.

3) Grow winter squash. If you've never grown winter squash before, be sure to give yourself ample time. The 1-5-year preparation time is an average, but it could take longer. First of all, squash are sprawling plants which require a fair amount of space, so you may need to save up to buy property, join a community garden, or lay claim to a piece of disused public land in the name of squash culinary curiosity … culinariousity. With the skyrocketing price of real estate, lengthy community garden wait-lists, and frank government disapproval of unilateral land grabs by the general populace, this part of the recipe is highly

unpredictable with respect to time. Even if you eventually secure enough earth in which to grow the squash, there is still the matter of, you know, growing it. You'll likely have to experiment with a few different varieties (there are dozens available) until you find one that grows, sets fruit, and ripens well in your region. I myself have had great success with acorn squashes, but that was after a couple of years of duds—a long time to keep my oven preheated. Common issues that arise while growing squash are pollination, powdery mildew, insufficient heat to fully ripen, and terrifyingly rampant and aggressive growth, such that it may be necessary to physically retreat from the hissing, sprawling vines and regroup before you even think about attempting harvest. Shoot, if you end up with a particularly vigorous grower, you may even be forced to surrender the land you waited so long for to the very squash you so eagerly sought to grow. Then it's back to the start of the recipe, I'm afraid. In that case, feel free to skip steps 1 through 3 and just order a pizza. Pizza's always good. If you are somehow able to wrestle a ripe squash from your leviathan vine, then for crying out loud, move on to step #4.

4) Roast the darned squash already.

The Plan

My fellow gardeners, you know: a vegetable garden does not grow itself. The rows do not magically align themselves, nor the seeds spontaneously burrow into the rows. The crops do not, of their own accord, enter into sensible rotations. No groups of community-minded veggies have organized a system of voluntary weed removal for the greater good of the garden. And to date, not a single salad has emerged fully formed from the earth to crawl, dressed, into my bowl.

I still set out bowls, just in case, but even I have come to accept that the growing of food takes hard work. It takes preparation. It takes experience and patience and stubbornness. Yes, it even takes a little luck. Above all, it takes a plan.

Well, I have a plan.

And it is a good plan. Do not doubt that it is a good plan. Do not, I beg, call into question the merit of this plan simply because it is not the first time I have claimed to have a plan. For who among us has not abandoned our intentions when reality descends upon the garden like so many raucous starlings? Spare me now your cynicism; this is not the place. See this plan for what it is, not for what the other plans failed to be. This plan is not those plans. This one is better.

It is a Garden Plan. Yes, like the others, but this time much bolder, far grander, drafted in pen with indelible ink, on good thick paper. Waterproof paper. Coffee-proof paper. Toddler-with-juice-proof paper. Where other plans were sketched in graphite by a hand febrile with thoughts of spring, only to be rubbed out by the coward's end of the old #2 pencil, this Plan, this one, is drawn to last. This Plan will not fall to the rubbery vacillation of its predecessors. It will not suffer death by a thousand erasings. It can't. For it cannot, in fact, be erased.

And why should it be? What possible cause for redaction could rear up and challenge the awesome rigor and vision of this Plan? Behold, its beauty, the fine clockwork majesty of its interlocking parts! Consider the peas—yes, look: this is where the peas will go. Three different varieties, with well-spaced maturation times. Once finished, they will be supplanted by beans, three more varieties, the better to assure a lengthy and robust harvest with enough breadth of taste and appearance to please the eye and palate both. These were selected to complement each other in growth habit, color, culinary application, and disease resistance. If I'm honest, one was selected principally because it's called 'Dragon's Tongue,' and that sounds hardcore.

But I'm getting ahead of myself.

This is just a small sample of The Plan's *legumes*. The same punctilious attention to detail in considerations of time, space, taste, and seasonal rotation has been applied to every category of crop independently, then laboriously integrated with all other crop categories with the help of supercomputers, spreadsheets … and the Circles.

Oh, did I mention the Circles?

No? You might want to hold on to something, then. This is where things get wild.

The Circles. First, they're not *really* circles. In the visual representation of the plan—some might say "map" or "layout," but these do not do justice—each sowing event is represented by a multidimensional shape. These shapes may, at times, under certain viewing parameters, superficially resemble circles. But, don't be fooled—again, they're not really circles. This is just one of those regrettable semantic shoehorns one must employ, cringing, with a concept that words fail. I could just as well have called them "Goofy Loops," but I didn't. Get over it. What do you want, an apology?

Each Circle, for each planting, symbolizes a set of values across a wide range of senses. These are expressed by colors, textures, temperatures, and musical tones according to such variables as sowing date, crop category, pest vulnerability, and fertilizer needs.

Mind blown yet? Hang in there.

The colors of The Plan's Circles are not limited by the human visual spectrum, because nature is not, and the musical tones produced by the circles change in pitch and volume as the season progresses and fertilizer needs change. The Circles can sing together, or they can collapse into a frantic dissonance. In addition, the normally cool bumps, ridges, and divots which comprise the textural element of the circles can sharpen or burn when dangerous combinations of certain plants and pests arise. Brussels sprouts + aphids, for example, might leave you with a papercut. Powdery mildew + any kind of squash is a Circle best avoided entirely. Just take my word for it.

Altogether, a perfectly executed garden becomes, through The Plan, a sensually harmonious, synesthetic symphony. On the other hand, a failing, languishing, or overly crowded garden will fall rapidly into a muddy, blaring din—sort of a nihilistic punk rock of angry Circles.

But—and I can't emphasize this enough—they're not *really* circles. Not by a long shot. As mentioned, these are shapes that simply cannot be rendered in two, three, or even four dimensions. It would be a bit like trying to depict a black hole and its effect on the fabric of space-time using nothing but sidewalk chalk. During a rainstorm. While doing a handstand. Inaccurate, to put it plainly. The requisite density of information is orders of magnitude greater than can be expressed through such frivolity.

Here again, in drafting The Plan, since higher-dimensional mathematics was not covered in any of my undergraduate botany courses, I deferred largely to supercomputers and a handful of generous, gullible grad students who somehow got it into their heads that I represented a freewheeling group of venture capitalists. Let it be known that I do not. But the mere suggestion of possible funding did produce some inspired work with respect to The Circles. At least, so I've been told. The truth is, no human's meager ration of sense organs can begin to perceive the Circles in their entirety. The grad students insist they are things of beauty, and I have little choice but to believe them. The broccoli Circles in particular, they say, look quite lovely in seven dimensions.

So yes, Circles, but not "circles." Goofy Loops, if you prefer. No other plan has them. This Plan does, and their scintillating perfection is a primary reason it will succeed. If, however, you are still in need of further evidence, allow me to delve a bit into the seed portion of The Plan.

You see, the seeds of The Plan have already been purchased. They are arriving daily. Each packet of seeds is checked in, entered into a database, briefed as to its role in The Plan, and then stripped of all useless labeling applied by the seed producer. Each parcel of seeds is repackaged and relabeled according to the superior classification system of The Plan.

Yes, it is superior. There is no hubris or boasting in my assertion that it is superior. It is merely a statement of fact. One does not boast about the rising of the sun. It is not folly to plan one's day on the assumption that the sun will rise again tomorrow. No, just like the sun, The Plan's seed-organization system exists in a sphere beyond arrogance and other petty human afflictions. Now, having mastered this superior method, I can't help but chuckle at other organization schemes as a knowing father smiles down upon his child attempting to smash a square block through a round hole. *Don't give up, little one, for we all once were infantile and new!* But, you know, also go ahead and try the round block before Daddy loses patience. No, the *round* one. Round!

Oh how we try, in our blockish innocence, to make the world accept whatever shape we hold in our hands.

Every gardener has struggled with it. How, for example, do *you* organize your seeds? Shoe boxes? Ziploc baggies? In that weird kitchen drawer with the cookie cutters and lighter fluid? Do not be ashamed, it's perfectly normal. You don't have to be proud, either, but go easy on yourself. Looking back, I cringe at my own flailing attempts to find order in the chaos. Envelopes and rubber bands and sharpies—oh, the bewildered adolescence of it all!

It all seems obvious now. For it was, in truth, such a simple problem to solve. All I had to do was apply the appropriate elements of cryptocurrency blockchain technology, The Dewey Decimal System, the APG IV system of plant taxonomy, and the good ol' Farmer's Almanac. Then I borrowed a bit of organic chemistry nomenclature to tidy up the modern mess of plant names. Et voilà.

(Try the round block, dummy, am I right?)

And just like that, I know where to find the exact seed I'm looking for. I know what to call it, and when to plant it.

Here we go, here's one: 2,3, dichlorocycloarrugulene ("arugula" to the layman). This lot of seeds should be back in the stacks, third floor, east wing, with the rest of the formally recognized Brassicales. Looks like I should sow after the next heavy rain when the moon is waxing. Piece of cake. It's a lot like your shoebox, only bigger and perfect.

Once each seed is sown the "transaction" is registered, appropriate blockchains are assigned, and the event is uploaded to the visual Plan in order to begin generating the requisite Circle. Excess seeds are then shipped to the

Svalbard Global Seed Vault where I have secured storage for them until such a time as my descendants or I are compelled by The Plan to sow again, which could be in two weeks or two hundred years. The Plan takes the long view on crop rotation. This extra storage step assures that each individual seed will maintain its precious viability for as long as possible, and none will be lost to the oblivion of the kitchen junk drawer. Generations from now, my descendants should be able to send for this leftover handful of arugula seeds and germinate them in whatever arable patch of earth remains to be cultivated.

Excessive, you may be thinking? Of course not! There is nothing excessive about The Plan. It is exactly what it needs to be. It cannot be reduced. After all, is a perfect, shimmering bubble "excessively" round? No! Attempt to remove any part of it, to "simplify" it, and the whole thing pops. Don't pop my Plan.

Besides, the effort is worth it; this is very good arugula.

It will, by this point, have been noted that the scale of The Plan is far too grand for any one person to manage. Certainly the administration and execution of The Plan requires a crack team of talented, devoted professionals who share my unique vision. And since my vision, at any given moment, is bound to be split cross-eyed between the minutiae of this sea change in the field of garden planning, and the necessary distractions of family—e.g., my son, playing with his blocks, who I now think is *intentionally* jamming that square block at the round hole just to spite me—this is no easy feat.

Such crack teams do not grow on trees, even when you're working with plants. So, in order to realize the astounding beauty, quality, and yields foretold by The Plan, I have taken three years to assemble under my command the crackest crack team you've ever seen. I have scoured the world for individuals possessed of that rarest and most synergistic combination of madness, brilliance, and subservience necessary to implement The Plan and grow a salad the *right* way. I now have at my disposal the finest computer scientists, theoretical physicists, theoretical agronomists, cryptographers, psychiatrists, chefs, graphic designers, massage therapists, lawyers, poets, engineers, yogis, dancers, biochemists, a klezmer band, and, just in case, a part-time gardener named Brian, who is paid by the hour. I may also have acquired a minor league baseball team somewhere along the way. I'll admit I got kind of caught up in the whole talent acquisition frenzy and saw some good young prospects in Arizona. Not sure yet how those guys fit into The Plan, but I'll put 'em to work. The catcher, anyway, seems wise beyond his years.

It is, dare I say, the new dream team. We are a veritable phalanx of fierce minds and ferocious attention to detail, armed with flow charts and clad in the impenetrable foresight of The Plan. Small-scale suburban agriculture won't know what hit it. Our mighty sword will slash a furrow in the earth from which will erupt a pyroclastic flow of fat, turgid gherkins and a billowing cloud of the darkest leafy greens.

Though in reality, we'll probably get Brian the gardener to slash a furrow in the earth while the rest of us stand back and cackle as a hail of cherry tomatoes slathers our faces with sweet pulp like the blood of our enemies.

No, no—it's all in The Plan. Trust me. See, right here, Article 15, Section 9: "like the blood of our enemies." I'm not making this stuff up. There is a reason for everything. For everything, there is a time, a place, a Circle, a Goofy Loop. There is a pulsing rhythm scored years in advance. It has already begun. It cannot be stopped or changed, only dutifully, joyfully voiced and succumbed to when each month and measure pass. Sing, Circles! Sing, seeds! Sing the glorious song of The Plan.

This is the only way now. There was nothing before the Plan. This is how my garden grows.

At least it will be as soon as Brian gets off break. I really should have made that guy salaried.

I wonder if any of those baseball players are any good with a hoe ...

Missing!

Chainsaw

Gently used. Late model. Left idling in the front yard after it bucked and scared the ever-loving bejeezus out of me one too many times. Someone may have taken it while I was cowering under the kitchen table.

But It's Okay!

Because I don't want it anymore! I'm done. I'm out. If found, or if you're the one who took the toothy, two-stroke demon, please, for the love of god, don't return it! Just keep the darn thing. May the both of you rot in hell. There isn't a branch in the world that needs pruning bad enough for me to pull that cord again.

Reward:

Oh … you'll get what you deserve.

New Plants Now!

S*queeee!* I'm so excited I can't stand it! It's my favorite time of the year, when I get to pull back the curtain at the annual New Plants Now! Conference and reveal what all those amazing plant breeders have been up to since we got tired of last year's introductions. That's right, it's time to dig up all your existing plants and toss them on the compost heap. They're not worth the NPK they're taking up. I've got new plants to tell you about. Better plants. Bigger plants. Likely much more *expensive* plants—but who cares?! They're called *royalties* for a reason: when you buy these babies, you'll *feel* like royalty. If you're not spending more than ever at the garden center, then I'm not doing my job!

No but seriously, uh, please buy these plants. I'll get fired if you don't, the people here are ruthless … please, just—

Heyheeeey! But on to the plants! Get out your wallet and your spade, your garden is about to get a high-fashion makeover. Here are a few of the standouts from the show. Keep in mind this short list represents just a fraction of what you can expect to be condescended to, for not having already heard of, by your gardening peers this season. It's darned near impossible to keep up, so if you get overwhelmed, just remember my golden rule of plant fashion: once it's in the ground, it's old news.

All right, let's dig in.

- **Amazeballs© Hydrangea. (*Hydrangea arborescens* 'Amazeballs2378436')**

The hydrangea arms race is over! 'Amazeballs' annihilates the competition with a multi-megaton explosion of white flower balls that will blast your puny human mind into a radioactive cloud of astonished, unworthy dust. But like, in a good way. It's simply stunning alone in the landscape, where its personal gravitational field may draw passing butterflies or smaller comets into orbit around its massive blooms. But also consider using cut flower heads as weapons to smite your enemies. Oh, you have enemies, trust me—and they're jealous of your 'Amazeballs' hydrangea. You just better buy one before they do.

- **Electric Fruitcake© Coral Bells. (*Heuchera* 'Elecfruccnzlbd9831')**

Look—just buy it, okay? We both know you can't tell the difference between any of these new heucheras, and this one's nothing special. Just write the name down and bring it to the nursery, they'll act impressed and take your money. That's how this works. "Enjoy" it for a couple weeks and then come back next month for your regularly scheduled heuchera obsolescence. By then the next cultivar in this series should be available; 'Midnight Fruitcake'©, anyone?

Oh—but I've said too much.

- **Limelight Common Dandelion. (*Taraxacum officinale* 'Limelion')**

With this most recent chartreuse offering, plant breeders have officially limelighted over 90 percent of the plant kingdom. I mean, what an achievement! You no longer have to settle for a *mostly* limelight garden; now every single plant can be limelight, weeds and all! What are you waiting for? Get out there and get your lime on. Also coming down the lime pipeline (limeline?), a spectacular new limelight quackgrass due out later this year—can't wait to spend an afternoon pulling *that* beauty out of one of my beds!

- **Vanishing Act© Coneflower. (*Echinacea x hybrida* 'Vanishing Act')**

Guaranteed to disappear faster than any other coneflower on the market! This new hybrid is drought tolerant, free-blooming, and won't ever come back no matter how much we call it a perennial. Stop your handwringing about whether that gorgeous echinacea you just shelled out big bucks for will return next year. This one definitely won't! In fact, if for some aberrant reason yours *does* poke its head up in spring, the breeders will send out a van to your garden and burn it with a weed torch. No more anxiety, no more wondering.

'Vanishing Act' is a rock-solid failure. There now, isn't that easier?

- **Balls-To-The-Wall© Hydrangea. (*Hydrangea arborescens* 'Ballstothewall38971')**

Waitwaitwait, okay—this, *this* is the hydrangea to end all hydrangeas. Forget that pathetic Amazeballs© impostor I mentioned at the beginning, the inflorescen—I mean, the *balls* on this new cultivar are TEN TIMES BIGGER. Holy *<bleep>*, that's big. If you bought the other one, sucks to be you, because this one's better. The stems can't even come close to supporting the weight of the balls, they just flop over and lie there in your garden like Jabba the Hutt. And I guess that's a good thing? Yes, I'm being told that's a good thing. So, show it off and brag about it, enjoy an inflated sense of confidence, but don't plant anything else nearby. Balls-To-The-Wall© was bred hungry and doesn't like competition.

- **Hardy Har-Har© Taro. (*Colocasia esculenta* 'Hardyhar631anko4')**

No, really, this one is definitely <*hehe*> completely, uh, "hardy." Yeah, <*snicker*> it's a <*mphh*> it's a hardy *Elephant Ear-WAAHAHAHAHA!* Sorry, I thought I could make it through without cracking. I know, I know—there's not a chance an elephant ear will survive the mere mention of real winter, but apparently you can claim any plant is "hardy" as long as you don't qualify what that means. I mean, I'm sure it's hardy *somewhere*, right? But oh man, so many people have fallen for it, you wouldn't believe. Or maybe you would, if you already bought one yourself. In any case, the breeder/marketing firm responsible is making millions, and that's what really matters. *Hooo*— "hardy." Oh, that's a good one.

• **Reverted Wonder© Box Honeysuckle.**
(*Lonicera nitida 'Reverted Wonder'*)

I ask you: What good is a beautifully variegated shrub if random shoots of new growth are continually reverting to the plain, boring old leaf color? Frustrating, right? Your garden, and by extension *you*, end up looking like you can't make up your mind! "Look at this place, Mary, I don't know whether these plants are supposed to be variegated, or not! The gardener must be a spineless hack. Let's bump him from the Horticultural Society posthaste." That's, uh … that's what they'll probably say if you've got wishy-washy foliage out there. Now, as we all know, Lonicera cultivars have been frequent culprits of this crime. But with the new 'Reverted Wonder,' a box honeysuckle has finally made up its mind! This one started out with the most stunning gold variegation—never burning, never bleaching in the sun—and then, like a miracle, the whole thing reverted overnight. <*Whoosh*> All of it. Yeah, foliage, I guess, goes <*whoosh*> when it reverts. Now you know. And it's terrific! I mean, it's just the plain old green now, but it's *all the same* plain old green. It's entirely pre-reverted, so you don't have to sit back and watch the poor thing vacillate between existential states like some tortured, shrubby chimera. "Good news, friend," your captious Hort. Society masters will probably say. "With 'Reverted Wonder' in your garden, we've decided you're back in the Society!"

- **Last Spine of Defense©® Home Security System. (*Agave spp.*)**

Well this is new. For the first time ever, we have a plant introduction from a home security company. For the last decade, these guys have been pushing millions of dollars into a hush-hush experimental plant-breeding program in order to produce a perfectly disguised, plant-based, home-defense system. Now that it has hit the market, they showed us some of the dead ends they pursued along the way: projectile-hurling shrubs; ensnaring vines; shrieking house plants; barberries. Pretty freaky stuff. Much of it involves some ethically questionable genetic engineering techniques they weren't too keen to discuss. In the end, the product they've released and shrewdly marketed is just plain old agave. No special breeding or science involved, you just buy an agave plant in one of their branded pots and stick it in front of any exterior door while you're away. The wicked spines on their leaf tips have proven to be a more effective deterrent of would-be crooks than any high-tech alternative they explored. Hey guys, I've got an idea: next time, maybe ask a horticulturist somewhere along the way. Any nursery worker with agave scars could have told you to start there.

- **Green Blob #9,783© Hinoki False Cypress.** (*Chamaecyparis obtusa 'Greenblob9783'*)

A distinct improvement over the previous 9,782 Green Blobs. Or so I've been told. Truly a quintessence of blobbiness, and undeniably green, but does it really come across as *greener* or *blobbier* in the landscape than, say, Green Blob #7,437©, which has always been my go-to blob? The breeders assure me that it does, though when I asked to see the new GB during the conference, the man just laughed and grabbed a random hinoki from a nearby table, saying, "Uhh, yeah, this one is … wait, what number are we on? Nine thousand?" After I provided him with the correct number, he laughed again, handed me the blob, and said, "Sure! Why not?!"

- **NoFuss© Ornamental Plum. (*Prunus cerasifera* 'Whybother34')**

A major breakthrough in the category of castrated fruit trees bred for low-maintenance landscaping use. Not only is the NoFuss© plum incapable of producing bothersome fruit, but its breeders have taken a giant leap forward by eliminating all those messy flowers *and* leaves in one fell swoop! Never again will the busy homeowner be forced to dodge useless and untidy blossoms as they shower gently to the ground in a spring breeze. No longer will neighbors quarrel about who must sweep up the burgundy tapestry of fallen leaves at season's end. And, as always, no gross, yucky, *food* dangling from the branches, thrusting sweet fruit onto innocent passers-by and staining the sidewalk below. Always nice and neat, sterile and austere, this "plum" is perfect for any gardener who is short on time and soul. No fruit. No flowers. No leaves ... NoFuss©. It's just a stick in the ground.

- **Some More Coleus. (*Solenostemon* etc., etc.)**

Oh, who am I kidding—I only made it about a quarter of the way through the eighty dozen or so new coleus introductions from *last* year. What chance did I have this time around? As soon as the plant breeders rolled out the coleus portion of their presentation my eyes glazed over, and I started meditating on nothingness. I do that sometimes. It wouldn't have been so bad—it's not like anyone *needs* more coleus to choose from—except a subvocalized "Om" came out a little more vocalized and exasperated than intended, and I was tersely asked to leave the convention center through the nearest exit if I couldn't be bothered to put my path to enlightenment on mute for a few minutes. To which I spluttered, I'm sorry to say, with a rather unenlightened sneer: "A few minutes?! If I sneak off to a week-long meditation retreat and check back, you windbags will only be halfway through the coleus! Find a new genus!"

And that pretty well wrapped up this year's installment of "New Plants Now!" I'm actually scribbling this down on a napkin in the parking garage because they wouldn't even let me back in to grab my laptop. I would say be sure to check back next year, but there's a distinct possibility that I will not be invited back to this particular conference. In which case, feel free to fill in the blanks yourself. Heucheras, coleus—

you know the drill. I trust you. If you end up broke and unsatisfied, you probably got it just about right.

As for me, maybe I will check out that meditation retreat after all. Is it just me, or has horticulture gotten *stressful?*

Recipes From My Garden

Forgotten Cabbage

Preparation Time: About 30 seconds, then aged ad infinitum.

Many cultures have traditional ways of preserving cabbage. Kimchi, sauerkraut, the possibilities are endless. I mean, that's two right there that I can think of off the top of my head, so the possibilities are at least two. Using such a rich dyad of available methods, wonderful flavors and eternal shelf life can be coaxed from our most humble, hardy, head-y veggie. It is with the utmost respect for, but frank unwillingness to attempt these techniques, that I submit my own cabbage-preservation recipe for consideration. With its emphasis on no-fuss preparation and indefinite storage, it should appeal to those busy gardeners among us who somehow managed to grow a cabbage but have no intention or realistic shot in hell of actually using it while fresh.

1) Hey, looky there! That cabbage you planted a while back actually grew! It's got a head and everything. Looks a little slug-chewed and misshapen, but you did it! Congrats. Color your thumb a shade greener and bask in your success. That's … I guess that's step one. So, do that. Bask away.

2) Now quick, pick it before something terrible happens to it! We'll come up with

a way to use it later, right?

3) Wash the cabbage, peel off the 14 outer layers of leaves that have been claimed in the name of King Aethwid the Earwig, and then put it in the crisper drawer of the refrigerator until you're struck by a vision of coleslaw so resplendent that it cannot be ignored.

4) When was the last time that happened to anyone, ever?

5) Meh. We'll put it in a soup or something.

6) But later, because this week is insane. The kids have dance class, swim lessons, and soccer. Whose ideas were they? I mean, the classes, not the kids. But since you brought it up ...

7) Look, it's just a matter of finding balance, is all I'm saying.

8) What's that supposed to mean? Too much time in the garden? We're trying to grow healthy food for the family, so we can be ... well, healthier, but we don't have any time to cook it much less eat it!

9) No no, you're right, soccer is much more important than nutrition. We just have to get the kids to graze some turf while they're out on the field doing wind sprints, so they don't DIE OF SCURVY!

10) I'm ... I'm sorry. That wasn't helpful. We'll do drive-through tonight and maybe figure out how to use the cabbage this weekend. Wooo—that'll be fun.

11) Sorry. I'll just stop talking. Forget I ever said anything about cabbage.

12) Wait 2-6 months

13) *Ugh*! Oh jeez, honey! What is this in the crisper drawer?

14) *Ooohh that's right* ...

As with all forgotten-veggie recipes, once the produce has been aged in the crisper drawer and then rediscovered months later, you can either grit your teeth and clean out the decayed remains, making room to start the whole process over, or quietly slide the drawer shut and pretend you never saw a thing. Which choice you make depends both on your intestinal fortitude and on how much you value the life you've built with your partner.

The Uprooted

O! There's no time for the hat! Leave it!"

"But—"

"Just GO! Runrunrun!"

<pant pant> "I don't ... understand! What happened?!"

"I'll explain when we ... get ... inside! Come on, in here! Hurry!"

"Let me just ... brush off my clogs real qui—"

"Dammit, forget about the CLOGS! Just get in here, it's right behind you!"

"Wh—AAAAHH! LET ME IN, LET ME IN!"

"Come on, quick, I got the door!" *<slam>*

<pantpant>

"Okay ... I think we're ... I think we're safe for now. So far none of them seem to be able to open a door."

"None ... none of *them*?! How many of those ... things are there? And what the hell are they? *Why* are they?!"

"Oh dear. I never should have invited you over to show you the garden. I thought they were all settled by now. I hadn't transplanted any of them for at least a week. Except ... well, except that, uh, that hinoki cypress that I moved to the front yesterday. But, but I *really* needed some more structure in that bed. You understand, right? I'm sure you move plants around all the time, all gardeners do, right? RIGHT? FOR THE LOVE OF ALL THAT IS HOLY, I CAN'T BE THE ONLY ONE THIS IS HAPPENING TO!"

"I ... I ... well, sure I relocate plants once in a while. But I don't understand—"

"Once in a while. Yeah, just once in a while, right? And that's okay, right? Like, *pffft,* no more than a few times a month, right? Nothing wrong with that, right? RIGHT?!"

"Wait, you mean you ... you move your plants around a few times a *month?*"

"Nononono. Not at all ... I mean, not *all* my plants. But, you know, some of them look good everywhere, some of them never seem to fit in, and you just can't decide where they should stay, so you try them a few different ... dozen different spots, until you get the perfect place and then you're happy! They're happy! It's perfect, right? But then, you know, sometimes I guess the plants get, I guess, well ... *confused* after being uprooted a bit too often and they, you know ..."

"No. No, I'm afraid I don't know. What?!

"Well, some of them ... they, uh, come unplanted, get up, and start ... walking around on their own?"

...

"What? Why are you looking at me like that?"

...

"Look, it's not *that* big of a deal, right? I'm sure this happens all the time."

"You're, you're describing plant ... *zombies*? No. No, I'm pretty sure that *doesn't happen all the time*! What's wrong with you?!"

"Oh ... oh dear ..."

"How many of them are there?"

"Well, it doesn't matter how *many* there are—"

"It *matters how many there are*!"

"*SHHHHH!*"

...

"Okay, okay, just keep your voice down. I don't know how many there are at any given time. Sometimes one will get up and just wander around for a while then plant itself again. Sometimes a couple will crawl over to the compost pile and jump on top—problem solved. And, well, sometimes one of them unearths a horde of minions and starts chasing you with a chainsaw from the shed."

"A *chainsaw*."

"Or—you know, whatever."

"O … kay. So on, like, a scale of one to chainsaw, how bad is this hinoki cypress with the hedge trimmers that just chased us in here?"

"Hard to say. The zombifers are an unpredictable bunch and—"

"*Zombifers?*"

"Yeah. You know, zombie-conifers."

"Oh, of course, I should have known. IS THIS SOME KIND OF JOKE TO YOU?!"

"Wh—no, not at all! It's *very* inconvenient. I spend days at a time in a makeshift bunker in my basement. I'm, I'm running low on wine, I've lost a thumb and a finger to a group of hell-bent hellebores, and I'm blind in one eye now, thanks to that gorgon agave I barely took down with the weed torch last week. Oh, and there's hardly any *wine* left."

"Yeah, you mentioned that—"

"Plus, most importantly, I can't be featured on the garden tour this year! Not with undead perennials on the loose now, can I? That's why I invited you over. I had to show *someone* my tree peony. This is the first year it's bloomed! Did you see it? I mean really, did you see it anywhere? It's gone AWOL. I heard it rustling around in the shed last night and I haven't seen it since. Oh, hey ... uh, you didn't bring any cabernet, did you? Maybe a pinot noir? I'm perilously low on reds."

"I'm ... a little ... upset that you invited me over to join in your, your private gardenocalypse ... without even warning me!"

"So no, then? No red wine? Well, god damn us then, this really is the end."

"Why ... why didn't you tell anyone?"

"I'm telling *you*, aren't I?"

"Only *after* one of your ... '*zombifers*' nearly severed my achilles! That is not fair warning! Why didn't you call the police or ... or the ... um, extension office or something? They might—"

"Shh! Hold that thought. We, uh, we might need to make another run for it here." <*BRRRRZZZZZZZ!*>

"Yeah, yeah—sounds like that hinoki managed to get the hedge trimmers back up and running. I mean, it'll *probably* do more damage to itself than us, but I'm … well, I'm running out of fingers. We'll go on the count of three, then?"

"What?! NO! Where are we going?"

"Here, light this, would you?"

"Is … is that a Molotov cocktail? Where did you—"

"Yeah. I can never manage to hit anything with these things, but they make a pretty good diversion."

"Well, that at least explains why your lawn looks like an artillery range."

"Shoot, you noticed? See, I would have been *so* embarrassed showing this place on the garden tour."

"I think people would maybe have noticed the plants chasing them with power tools—"

"Oh hush. Okay, really, though, I do need to throw this. So, let's go NOW! FOLLOW ME!"

"Wh—AAAAHHHH!"

<*KABOOOOM!*>

"THIS WAY, QUICK, TO THE BASEMENT!"

70

"*EEEEEEEE!*"

"Oh my god, I got it. I hit it!"

"*EEEEOOOOOO!*"

"How is it making that noise! It's a conifer, not a—"

"Zombifer!"

"Fine! It's a *zombifer*, that doesn't mean it has *vocal chords!*"

"*EEEEAAAAAAOOOOO!*"

"Uh—it's, it's not stopping. It's not stopping! Go, go, go!"

"*Where?!*"

"Bunker! I mean, basement! Basement bunker! Just go!"

"*EEEEWWWWHYYYY?!*"

"Did—did it just ask *<pantpant> why*?!"

"Well, *<pantpant>* why not?"

"I, *<pantpant>* hate, *<pant>* your garden!"

"Oh, you do not! *<pantpant>* Hey look! There's the tree peony! *<pantpant>* Isn't it lovely?"

"It's *<pantpant>* it's got a line-trimmer!"

"Yes, but look at the *size <pantpant>* of those blooms! Ahhh! Quick, in here!"

"AAAHHHH!"

<Slam>

"I … didn't know *<pantpant>* peonies were so *fast!*"

"Yeah ... I think it's a little *<whew>* annoyed that I tried to move it while it was blooming."

"You tried to *transplant* your tree peony while it's *in bloom*?! What's the matter with you?"

"Well I know you're not *supposed* to, I'm not an idiot, I just really wanted those enormous blooms front and center for the garden tour, and you could barely see it in the back—"

"You're not *on* the garden tour! Your garden has gone all ... unholy, psycho, living dead because you won't leave it alone! Just sit back for a minute and try to enjoy your garden as it is without moving something around!"

"But ... but how is that *gardening*?"

"You prefer *this*? Aren't you maybe finding this a *little bit* stressful? Just let your plants live the life they've got without your ... divine intervention every other day. Who cares if the garden *looks* perfect for the garden tour if it's actually miserable and wants to kill you?"

"Well ... I guess *I* do."

<Sigh> "I ... I think I need a drink. Did you say you're *completely* out of wine down here?"

"No, not entirely. I've got a bottle of ... let's see—port, ugh—and some whites, I guess."

"Too bad. Hmm, you know … you know who always brings good red wine?"

"Ooh, Susan!"

"Susan."

…

"Do you suppose … I mean, don't you think Susan would want to see your spectacular tree peony in bloom for the first time?"

…

…

"*EEEEEEOOOOOWWWWWHYYYYY?!*"

"I mean, we could at least call and invite her, right?"

Missing!

Gardening Clogs

Urgent! Please help. Well-worn, but beloved pair of gardening clogs has been missing for a week. It's spring! I've got planting, sowing, weeding—there's SO MUCH to do outside, but instead I'm stuck in the house.

My wife told me to "just put on a different pair of shoes."

Like, what, I'm supposed to muck around the perennial bed in my tennis shoes?

I'm a gardener, not a savage.

I need my clogs!

Bring them here.

Paralyzed

I can't move.

A pillow, hot against the side of my face, threatens to swallow me up. There would be worse ways to go, but still. I'm in bed. And I can't move.

My eyes creak open on sleep-rusted hinges. Everything is blurry, but what looks to be an enormous seed catalog lies splayed on the nightstand, inches away, looking guilty. Awareness trickles in like something too long held at bay, about to burst.

I'm in bed. And I can't move. And I'm an idiot.

The still-dark morning wraps tight around me. I'm thrashed-up and tangled in sheets, with sweat beading on my brow, beading everywhere really, that sweat can. Whatever pitched battle raged through my sleep took its toll, and it's not over yet. The air is thick with unfinished business. Fat drops of doubt fall heavy, portending deluge from an unseen storm. Angst and indecision carom and clang in my gut like some crazy pinball bonus round. They've been at it all night. My stomach is decidedly *not* paralyzed.

I blink. I groan. I still can't move.

It shouldn't be a surprise, to find such unrest within me. Dark clouds were looming even before I slept: ominous, billowing towers pushed high by a turbulent psyche. Occasional strobes of lightening flashing on pieces of war, grinding into place behind my eyes. The phantom drone of distant engines throbbing along the storm front, inbound. A four-star curry heartburn hollering at me from dinner, doing nothing to broker peace.

And all this turmoil wrought by an avoidable mistake, a late-night indulgence that would paralyze come morning. A gardener's stupid gluttony.

That damned seed catalog.

I should have known better.

Plants Are Terrible People

It is winter, some faceless month in winter, when the nascent shoots of spring beckon from across a wide gulf of cold, dark days, and the fresh taste of summer's harvest has long since slithered off like a dream chased. These are the doldrums, the boundless empty sea between seasons. It's enough to drive a gardener mad. Desperate, we scan slack sails for the slightest hint of warm breeze to carry us through to the other side. Days like these need a bit of hope, some beam of borrowed sunshine, a reason to put on pants in the morning.

Mine came in the mail yesterday.

No, not the pants. Hope. For what did I find but that bright herald of good things to come: the seed catalog! Salvation! Rolled up with coupons for garage-door-repair and eleven or so credit-card-offers, a magnificent book of dreams hummed a muffled overture to rebirth, right there in my mailbox.

It was a good catalog too—one of my favorites: a great, thick tome of vegetable seeds and supplies. It flaunted page after page of evocative descriptions and photos—lascivious tomatoes and tantalizing brassicas; simpering squashes and exotic salad greens; beans. Everything to drive a deprived gardener wild with desire. I saw asparagus and I laughed, carrots and I was moved to tears, kohlrabi and—well, I'm not fond of kohlrabi, but darned if it doesn't look enticing when the rain is coming down sideways and the sun sets at noon. Even the pictures of celery were nice enough to temporarily suppress flashbacks of the wretched steamed celery fed to me as a kid.

I was hungry. I wanted it all.

But you all know how this goes. I couldn't put the thing down. Whether your vice is vegetables, bulbs, rare perennials, or exotic annuals, if you call yourself a gardener you know what that first catalog of the year meant to me: seed season had begun.

And just in time. Winter had overstayed its welcome and this was my excuse to kick that freeloader to the curb. *Sorry, Winter, I've got a whole bunch of little friends coming over, and they always bring salad. Now get the hell off my couch.* Oh, the satisfaction. There was an electric urgency I felt when I held the seed catalog, a euphoria. It was my ticket back to a place where something besides stoic leeks and seasonal affective disorder might grow.

That's why last night, in a swirling delirium of choices, I brought it ... to bed.

I know, I know—what was I thinking? What did I expect would happen? But I couldn't resist. I was silly with the possibilities. Clutching a flashlight as though it were all some harmless bit of childhood mischief, I flipped pages deep into the night. I considered and calculated. I speculated. I argued with myself—that fool—and myself argued back.

Runner beans vs. bush beans? Snow peas or snap? What on Earth was to be done about kale? And good lord, what a glory of radishes! I don't even like radishes, but wow! All those permutations, all the potential, each combination of seeds promised unique riches and delights in a bounty that boggled the mind.

It was too much, of course—too much titillation, too much fantasy. My garden is small, there would never be room enough for it all. But on the cusp of sleep, the thunderheads of reality always look soft and far away. Any garden seems possible when glimpsed beneath the covers at midnight, lit by the soft headlights of dreams. All restrictions fall away as downy fluff, and every practicality giggles off to nothing. The only limitation is what you can't make-believe. There's always time enough to play before the storm.

But the playground upon which I unleashed my imagination was to become, overnight, with no conscious chaperone, a battlefield. At some point, hypnotized by the options set before me, I dozed off, all those seeds dancing like soporific sugar plums in my head. The catalog slid to the nightstand, and whichever minor god of mischief got assigned to gardening snickered from its underworld in glee.

Because sometime during the night, a sour, unpleasant truth must have burbled up into the well of my subconscious. An infectious little bastard bug of the obvious, which skittered around to all corners of my mind, hissing: *Choose carefully, for there can be only* one *garden this year.*

And it was right. I can't have everything. However many coveted seeds might survive the selection process and make it onto the order form, tenfold more must slip into the rough-tilled rows of could-have-been. Most will not make the cut, no matter how intriguing or promising they might be. The furrow is only so deep, the season only so long. The vegetable garden is a zero-sum game.

Once that realization spread, it was only a matter of time before battle lines were drawn. Throughout the forsaken hours of morning, what began as a playful celebration of choice descended unconsciously into debate, then argument, then fisticuffs, and finally, a call to arms, to throw down and fight for the future of the sprouts that will or won't burst proudly from the earth this year. War cries and sirens rang out through the night, a riotous internal din which scored my fitful sleep. I can't imagine my wife slept well, either. But that's what she gets for marrying a gardener.

Now, the morning after, flashes of waking consciousness illuminate the battlefield; a scarred terrain of mind. A full-on war is being fought here: a great and terrible War for the Seeds. Subconscious factions have already dug in and reinforced their positions before I could even wake to take sides. They are aligned by root vegetable preference, by hotness of pepper, by willingness to indulge the long ripening times of shallots. For some reason, there's a rabid group especially opposed to shelling peas, another to beets. Nobody seems to want parsnips this year, but their virtues are being vehemently attacked and defended anyway.

And I'm stuck lying in bed in the middle of it all. No man's land. Mortar shells explode around me, within me. On all fronts, the heavy artillery of opinion and zeal whistle down and carve booming craters in the landscape.

<EEEEEYYYYYYYOOOOO KA-BUSHBEANS!>

I guess some part of me really wants bush beans.

Shrieking air support swoops in on hot jets of fury, passion, and blind conviction, its payload full of emotional shrapnel meant to tear through the enemy's expressed fondness for cauliflower. Collards are grappling with mustard greens. Scallions and leeks have thrown down. Cucumbers are dance fighting. Tomato cultivars whistle overhead as cover fire for a solanacious advance.

Brandywine! Sungold! Stupice!

And suddenly there are eggplant afoot.

There's nowhere I can run, no asylum to be had, no Switzerland of the mind to duck into while things settle down. Because it's all happening inside me, splinters of my own self colliding over trifles, with no regard for my conscious authority in the matter.

And all I want to do is climb out of bed and get some coffee.

Pffft—authority. Who am I kidding? I have no authority anymore. There is no jurisdiction here; there are no respected borders in this kind of dispute. A garden grows from the gut and the heart as much as from the head. It is senseless and stubborn and passionate, a loose alliance of urges with uncommon goals and unspoken motives, too factious and numerous to ever reach lasting accord. I left myself vulnerable to a coup the moment I dropped the catalog and started snoring. The coals of discord were glowing and what did I do? I fanned them to flame with a hundred pages of heirloom seeds and then nodded off like a senile dictator too cocksure of his own primacy to ever suspect a fire could burn without his permission. I yawned all through the warning signs and was sawing logs by the time the first skirmishes broke out. So maybe I deserve this.

The worst sort of conflict is that within a person. And mine is fought annually. Each winter the bickering starts. Which seeds to buy? Which outfit will the garden sport? For which precious few of the thousand varieties available will I poke a hole this coming spring? How many heirlooms, how many hybrids, how many new introductions with trademarked names will be selected, to show up in my mailbox like shell-shocked soldiers who have survived the ordeal but at what cost? How many more will remain alluring strangers to my soil, to pile up in that great logjam of regret that snarls my every memory now and forever. Years from now their catalog photos will haunt me, like old school crushes from yellowing yearbooks. *<Sigh>* Oh, watermelon *radishes, you didn't really* taste *like watermelon, did you?*

And how on earth to decide, to narrow the choices? Checklists, charts, careful notes, highlighters, blindly thrown darts? A process. A system. A method.

All have failed, in their own way.

The dilemma has been bitten, gnawed, torn apart, and abandoned to the slavering dogs of the id, who have gone berserk with the smell of blood—sorry, seeds. The smell of seeds. This has become a very violent metaphor.

But there is a breed of violence to this struggle. If the wrong selections are made, if the insurgent, traitorous radicals have their way and sneak impossible cantaloupes onto the order form again, there *will* be casualties, measured in lost yield and pride. Innocents like my children will be robbed of the unknown, tasty joy a more successful alternative crop might provide. And oh, the shame when there are no fresh, sweet carrots for the kids' school lunches because some impulsive fool just had to try pac choi instead.

How would *you* like a handful of pac choi in your lunch?

It's a fate I'd not wish on anyone. *Someone* must defend the unknown Tasty Joy. Someone must endure the trials and torments of indecision. Someone must think of the children and put their foot down when pac choi comes calling.

Well this is my garden, and that someone is me.

Or it was, until I pulled the pin on this seed grenade and then handed it off to my shifty-eyed, subliminal lieutenants for safekeeping while I went ni-nite. Now, the firestorm raging in my head will burn until the last bean is standing, until the traumatized order is placed. There's nothing I can do but observe with horror the free-for-all I've unleashed. A month from now, the seeds will come in the mail and I'll be on the outside, looking in, unable to vouch for or to remember any of it. Who chose Chinese yard-long beans? Which faction made the case for corn? We don't have room for corn! And dammit, I'm not growing kohlrabi again, I'm just not.

Or so I'll say, but to the victors go the spoils.

Meanwhile this morning, yes, I am still paralyzed. I can't get up and start the day without stumbling into the minefield that was laid while I slept. Any step, any movement, could be interpreted by the warring tribes in my head as implicit support for an enemy faction's hated propaganda. Were I to swing my legs down to the carpet at the wrong moment, during a potato brawl, for example, it might be met with howls of rage that I would dare step in to side with the fingerlings.

Noooo! Not those shriveled finger-frauds, how could you?! The pro-russet forces would explode in my skull until I relented and flopped back to the pillow. I'd have to try a different tactic. Or a different potato.

So the morning goes. I'm entrenched. Stuck. Sick of fighting with myself over seeds, but unable to stop. I know I need to get out of bed, but not until this is settled. Hours pass before my mind suddenly goes quiet. An eerie calm settles like a fog within me. Is it a cease-fire? A trap perhaps? Or, has the war left no survivors? Is every part of me now so sick of the bickering and rage that I've lost all will to plant?

Only one way to find out.

I sit up in bed. Fearing the worst, I reach slowly for my slippers. Put them on. Stand up. So far so good. Maybe the war has run its course, diplomacy taken hold. Maybe I'll be able to calmly and rationally order a few seeds. Keep it simple, keep it civil. Whatever crops I grow this year, they will be enjoyed and appreciated for what they are, and not what they could have been.

A cautious and hopeful serenity dawns in me as the first rays of sunlight peek through the blinds. Outside, a chickadee's song signals peace. I have survived, and I will be stronger for it. With a long, deep breath I bend to pick up the seed catalog spread open on the nightstand, culpable but shameless.

My breath catches as the pictures exposed on the open page resolve through my bleary eyes. I recoil with a cold dread at what I see, but it's too late.

A battalion of lettuces stares up at me from the page.

It's an ambush.

Fire!

Buttercrunch this, you dogs!

All right, soldiers, it's loose-leaf or no leaf, now get out there and—

I want those impure mescluns out of our garden!

Romaine?! No-maine! Romaine?! No-maine—

What the unholy hell is radicchio?!

Cut-and-come-again, cut-and-come, cut-and-come, cut-and—

I'll hoe your toes before I allow a worthless iceberg in here!

Sorrel, you sour, sorry weed this is the last time you—

Bibb to the bitter end!

Oh, screw it. I don't have time for this, I'll just order all of them.

Recipes From My Garden

Four-Alarm Kale Chips

Every kale chip aficionado—and I think there are as many as nine of you now—knows all too well that a couple of things can go wrong when crafting your snack of choice. The kale winds up either (a) soggy from too much oil or, (b) black and burned from overcompensation for (a). Both maladies render the chips unpleasant and barely edible. Which is only a little worse than successful kale chips, but since we're working with very little margin for error, it's best to avoid either fate.

My approach, instead of striving for that (still unsatisfying) textural middle ground between the two extremes, is to embrace both at the same time. The following recipe will, hopefully, achieve a precarious culinary balance by averaging out equal parts sog and char. Kind of like if you were to revive that burnt, utterly carbonized marshmallow that no one around the campfire wants by soaking it in a bowl of olive oil overnight. Brilliant, right? Why wouldn't it work for kale too? It'll be great. So, the keys to this recipe are going to be lots of oil, lots of fire, for a long time. What could possibly go wrong?

1) NOPEnopenopenope. Don't do it, bad idea—burned the kitchen down, still tasted awful.

2) Hey, you know what are great? Potato chips.

On Fire

Your garden is on fire. The whole thing, it's burning down. OMG. Never mind how it started, never mind how it's possible. It doesn't matter. There's no time. It's a sky-high, five-alarm, botanical bonfire. Look, there go your azaleas—*poof!*—and the gardenias too. The whole garden is suddenly blooming at once, in gaudy orange petals of flame. Its fragrance is powerful. You're gasping for air, which suddenly seems in short supply. The smoke is unbearable, rich with the miasma of burning flowers.

Have you ever smelled burnt lilies before? Well, you're about to.

Quickly now, grab a shovel! You have decisions to make. Because you can't save everything. It may be that you can't save much of anything. Especially if you don't get moving.

Don't think about it, just go! What are you going to do? Which plants will you try to rescue? Is there anything so precious out there you would willingly brave a hell storm in order to rescue?

Your house is fine, don't worry about that. Your family, your cats and dogs, they are all fine. They're in town, bowling or something. Yes, without you. I don't know, maybe because you always complain about greasy bowling-alley food. Don't worry about it, they're safe. You hate bowling, what do you care?

The fire department has been notified; they are on their way. Sirens wail in the distance: a thin sound with far-off good intentions—no good to you at the moment. Here and now is the roar, the crackle and hiss of your vision and hard work going up in smoke. It is the din of things coming undone, a keening unrehearsed by any, but known by all. It spreads like a flash mob, dancing through the garden as each plant joins the infernal choir in turn.

But don't expect the firefighters to care about your plants. Nor should they, really. Imagine the outrage if it were discovered that the whole neighborhood burned down while a full fire company charged into your garden with shovels to help you lift your peonies. Yes, sorry, I know you have some lovely ones out there—even an old tree peony—but can we agree their salvation is maybe not the highest priority of local emergency resources?

If you want to save that tree peony, then *you* have got to save that tree peony.

So, do you? Is your peony the crown jewel you simply can't bear to part with? I know, I know, its blooms are the size of your face. *And* fragrant. It's a treasure, believe me I get it. "Local Gardener Found Charred, Clutching Peony." It would make a tragic headline, but I'd understand completely. Few others would, but by this point you should have come to terms with the limited range of sympathy afforded by outsiders for gardeners meeting the natural consequences of their actions. Your family, for example, may have preferred you saved your own stupid butt instead of the peony, which probably won't survive the emergency transplant anyway. Now they will have nothing. They will be scarred. They will never bowl again.

If not your life, then, what *would* you risk to save your favorite plant from this fiery fate? Is there a hibiscus so cherished you would suffer agony in its defense? An iris worth disfiguring burns? Chapped lips for a fuchsia? Would your rare, hardy schefflera warrant an ambulance trip to the ER if it meant you could save it? That thing came all the way from Taiwan, after all. Even so, do you have any idea how expensive an ambulance trip to the ER is? Have fun explaining *that* bill to your family. *Sorry guys, no bowling for the rest of the decade while we pay off these medical bills. At least the schefflera made it, though, am I right? Did you know that thing came all the way from—*

Yes, good luck finishing that sentence and staying married.

Hurry now, you have got to save *something*. As we speak, the old arbor you love so much seems to have been caught in a highly localized magma flow. No, I don't think your annual coat of weather sealer is going to offer much protection in this case. And as for the climbing rose that was growing up the arbor, its prospects don't look good either. As far as I know, there's no USDA Hardiness Zone that covers active volcanoes.

It took so long to train that rose. You suffered so many punctures, scratches, and minor skin infections as its thorns protested your ham-handed treatment. Now, the fruit of all your pain and hard work is going up in smoke.

And it's only just beginning. Think of all the time you have invested in this garden over the years. Think of the sheer force of creative will and man/woman power you have summoned to coax a lush paradise from whatever neglected lot preceded it. It took everything you had. It was the best you could do. Now, ash to ash, weeds to weeds, all of it is returning to the ground as fertilizer for the next round— which is an admirably positive way of looking at things, but one that has not likely crossed your mind.

Has *anything* crossed your mind? I only ask because you don't seem to be moving. At all.

Perhaps you are stuck wondering if it will even make a difference. Could the handful of plants you might save ever amount to anything more than keepsakes, like so many strands of hair in a locket? Will the garden itself live on through them? Do they have a chance of preserving the memories of all those sunny spring afternoons with dirt under your nails? Of untold time spent carving something beautiful from this small hollow of the Earth? Will these refugees speak of the first time your apple tree bore, or the snap pea seedlings your daughter checked daily, or the filthy gloves you threw at your spouse when they turned the hose on you? Or, will it hearken instead only to this fateful day, when the daffodils went off like a string of firecrackers?

Either way, you would be asking a few traumatized perennials to shoulder the burden of representation for a much greater thing that was lost. Would you really expect them to carry on as though nothing had changed, or, at least, to carry on as though the changes were bearable? It seems like a lot to ask of a peony.

After all, you yourself certainly won't be the same after this. Not by a long shot. The context of your life will have changed. The garden, having accompanied you for so long, had become a convenient framing device for who and what you were. It grew with you. It tilted with your seasons and spoke your shared time in fearful whispers at sunset. It was your contrast and your complement. It wrapped you in strong tendrils and now ...

Well, who are you without it? What is your life in a wreath of charred stems?

I can't say I know, but I do know that you are dithering. Hemming *and* I daresay hawing. This is no campfire; there are no s'mores to be had when the coals burn low. Isn't there *anything* you care to preserve? It's not like you just drove to the nursery one weekend on a whim, loaded up whatever plants they had on sale, and then dumped them in the backyard proclaiming "Garden!" A collection like this took *time.* (And money too, more than you'd like to admit—but think of the *time.*) Yes, there are a few sale-rack finds out there, but also the hard-won spoils of years spent lurking at garden centers on delivery day, waiting on call-me lists, scouring online and mail-order catalogs, stalking community plant sales, hoarding rare seeds of questionable origin, and surreptitiously taking cuttings in direct violation of neighborly trust and modern patent law.

All of it is on fire. Right now. What part of this are you not understanding? You, whose feet seem stuck in cement, are you giving up? Have you so quickly resigned yourself to roasting hot dogs and starting over tomorrow from scratch?

Or, will you not start over after this? Will this ruinous fire prove to be the proverbial straw that burned the camel down? (Don't worry about it—it's a new take on the proverb.) Perhaps your very will to garden is being oxidized and commuted to vapor and coal in the same furnace of fiery breath that is devouring your garden itself. Never again shall you don vest and clogs, nor wear holes in pants-knees, or callus the tips of your fingers. Because whatever joy or satisfaction that once compelled you to do so has fizzled away in this, your own backyard tithe to the inevitable heat death of the cosmos. Cue slow motion shot of you, The Gardener, walking away, your face and soul hard forged in the uncaring furnace of dreams that rages behind you, raising a charred hot dog to your mouth and stabbing forward a flaming marshmallow into the darkness of tomorrow—

Or not. There you go now making a move for your hepaticas. I had a feeling you would come back for those. Folks who are into hepaticas are *really* into hepaticas.

So, great, you've saved an armful of your precious liverleaf babies, now what? While you were doing that, the berry patch over there met with a sudden and violent pyrotechnic end. It was impressive and almost beautiful: part fireworks show, part funeral pyre, and part strawberry shortcake flambé.

What in the *world* is going on out there? It is hard to imagine what you may have done to anger the gardening gods so, or understand why, in this instance, their wrath is visited with such apocalyptic fury. Usually they are a pretty passive-aggressive bunch. Aphids, downy mildew, blossom-end rot—these are the customary arrows in their smiting quiver. True, there was that one time my own lawn caught fire, but said incident likely had less to do with divine fury than with my ill-advised use of a weed torch in August. No, you must have committed an act so appalling to the unseen forces of horticulture that it could not be ignored.

Oh wait—I know what it was. It was the unsanctioned taking of cuttings I mentioned earlier, wasn't it? Yes, sorry, the gardening pantheon came down squarely on the side of plant breeders in the matter of patent infringement. I Bet you're wishing you had bothered to find out what the "PPAF" on all those plant tags meant. *Huh? Asexual propagation prohibited. I wonder what that means.* I don't believe you. You know what it means. You sure as heck didn't grow all those flashy new delphiniums from seed, I know that much. Now they're cursed and burning with everything else. Patent pending nevermore.

Or, maybe it was something else. Failing to deadhead your annuals? Disturbing a magnolia's roots? Improper layering of your compost pile? All of these are likely to raise the bile of vengeful minor deities. Wait a minute—you didn't prune a

Group 3 clematis like a Group 1 clematis, did you? Lord, if so, you had better start begging for mercy right now.

Later, perhaps when your garden lies more comfortably in smoldering ruins and less in open flame, you can ask yourself in a ruminant sort of way if the reason for all this devastation even matters. Whether your patch of earth was smote by capricious gods, or made the punchline of one of the universe's many unfunny jokes, the end result is the same. And in this case, it smells like barbecue gone horribly wrong.

Perhaps the fault was your own for caring too much in the first place. You clung tightly to your little leafy entourage, you loved them so. What did you think would happen when their brittle tinder met the flames of the world? Surely you must have suspected that, by time or by fire, the things you held closest would burn you the deepest. And if you didn't? Well, consider this blaring smoke alarm your overdue wakeup call. (Sorry, no, once it starts no one knows how to shut it off.)

The choices before you then, while more urgent with the heat on your face, are no different than anyone's: you can drop everything and walk away, far enough from life's sparking bits to never again risk the inevitable immolation of love, or you can hold fast to your old garden friend, and with singed hair and red eyes know that, for what it's worth, you were together until the end.

Hey, no one said it was an *easy* choice.

But, since one of your roses over there just exploded into thorny smithereens, I would try to reach a decision sooner rather than later. Wow, I can't say I've ever seen such a thing before—the exploda-rose. That's a new one. At least, it wasn't covered in Plant Pathology 101. Looked like one of your grandifloras, but I couldn't see very well—there was a lot of shrapnel in the air. Maybe it was just a rugosa. I suspect most roses look similar while exploding.

See, this is the sort of thing that's *not* supposed to happen to a garden, right? Spontaneous combustion of roses in particular yes, but also, more generally, this breed of random, inexplicable violence to which we as people are more typically vulnerable. Gardens are meant to be more robust, enduring institutions. They are supposed to outlive their gardeners, to be passed on in perpetuity through a succession of earnest caretakers in loving memory and fidelity until such a time as—

Oh, come now, you didn't really believe all that did you? Maybe you didn't expect *this* level of carnage, but certainly you suspected it would be a long shot that your garden might end up in the hands of anyone able to recognize your vision, much less to tend and preserve it. Sure, your plum tree might have survived a changing of the guard—that is if it hadn't been scorched by that flock of fire-breathing sparrows that just passed through—but the odds that any bereaved inheritor or future homeowner would know what a Hepatica *was*, much less what to do with one, were never great. As soon as you're gone, they are sodding over the lot, and you know it. They need more lawn. Somewhere for the dogs and kids to run around. Plus, whatchama-paticas might be poisonous or something. Or, you know, hypothetically, what if the roses started exploding? Gardens can be downright *dangerous*. Better safe than sorry.

Between such ignoble fates then, what is the meaning of it all? What will it matter that you loved a lily, that you were proud of your poppies, if you either live to see them burn before their time or know with your own last breath that you won't be around to save them next time?

It meant everything. And nothing.

Because those are the only two sides of this coin we're flipping. And however it lands, we only have the one coin. It might be hard to see, through all the smoke. But then, the world is always on fire. Can you at least now, with your own garden ablaze, see that life itself is one glorious cremation, full of brightly burning flowers, made no less beautiful for the ash it smears across our hearts? You can either come close and warm yourself or shiver off alone.

So how about this: Heads, you take a deep breath, charge into that inferno, and grab every plant you can until there's no more air in your lungs. Or, tails, you go back in the house and wait for those faraway sirens to come.

Go ahead, flip the coin.

I can't look.

<u>Missing!</u>

<u>Blueberries</u>

My blueberries are gone! All of them.

Please, if you have any information regarding their whereabouts, contact me immediately.

I've been waiting for years for my plants to mature enough to produce a good crop, and this year they finally did. These bushes were loaded with fruit just this morning.

No way did birds or rats get to all of 'em that fast.

Plus, the kids were running around the yard most of the day, they would have scared off any—

Oh, right …

<u>Never Mind!</u>

If you see a couple of little purple-faced, human blueberries rolling around and groaning, please notify them that tummy aches are just desserts for a berry binge.

Let's Euphemize!

My garden is _____. And so very _____. It is the most _____ place in the world to me and brings no small measure of _____ every time I gaze upon it. You wouldn't believe how _____ it is, or how many _____ I have. I couldn't be more _____ of all the _____. Oh, and the _____! Well, let's just say I have a way with _____. _____, on the other hand, those _____-ing _____-s I could do without.

Yep, that's my garden.

Before I go filling in the blanks here though, let me just confess that I don't quite know what to tell you about my garden. Not that you asked, but believe it or not folks occasionally do. Customers, coworkers, neighbors, social media acquaintances—they will drop simple, innocent inquiries about the nature of my garden, delivered with all the gravity and sincerity of a "How's it going?"

Fine.

"So, what's your garden like?"

It's fine. Thank you.

Does anyone *really* want to know how it's going? Likewise, does anyone care that the soil in my front yard is always impossibly dry and root-choked because of two huge deciduous trees which are tolerated solely because their trunks are conveniently spaced one hammock-width apart, and I'm not about to spend my summer hammockless like some barbarian?

Perhaps not, but I care. And that's why I find myself at a loss for words when asked. Because while I am fiercely proud of my little space and all the hard work I've put into it, I am almost as fiercely disappointed by it. It is disheartening that all the hard work I've put into it has not resulted in something more closely resembling an "after" photo than its "before" counterpart. Together, my garden and I are at least a couple of musical montages short of the big reveal. (Sidenote: does anyone know where I can order one of those montages?) As it is, every time I glance outside, I am nearly slapped silly by hard-hitting questions for which I have no answers.

Whatever happened to those five hundred daffodils I planted three years ago? *<slap>*

Why can't I grow a hellebore that doesn't act like a sullen teenager? *<slapslap>*

Who planted all these confounded heathers? *<slapslapheadbutt>*

That was me, I planted the heathers. And ouch.

It's easy enough to pin the garden's shortcomings on a lack of sufficient time, money, and energy to unify the dozens of ideas that have been splattered all over the lot like a sneeze. And fair, to some extent. But if I'm honest—and let us assume that's the case here, anyway—it is just as accurate to state that my garden falls short of magnificent because I don't know what I'm doing. After all these years, I still find myself floundering and flailing, in over my head in the deep end of the garden design pool. Which isn't even all that deep, as far as pools go; I'm just not a great swimmer.

Even if an unencumbered six months fell into my lap, gift wrapped, with a blank check and a card reading: *Go, make your garden. Sincerely, The Universe*, I would probably spend five and a half months on a reckless plant-buying binge, followed by a few days of hyperventilating in raw, unproductive panic. Think *Fear and Loathing in Las Vegas*, but with hydrangeas. After everything, I'd probably have *more* heathers, and the hellebores and I still wouldn't be on speaking terms.

As I have come to learn the hard way, there is a wide chasm separating your common horticulturist from a talented Creator of Gardens. And it goes beyond capital letters. As a representative of the former group who often finds himself in the company of the latter, can I just say this is quite irritating? It really gets under my skin. Come on, I know a *lot* of plant names; I can easily discern a Petunia from a Calibrachoa; I know what an intergeneric hybrid is! Shouldn't I be able to translate all this useful knowledge into a beautiful garden? Once an art student learns the names of the colors, doesn't the canvas pretty much paint itself?

Okay, who all is still reading? Did all the landscape architects and art students just storm out in a huff? Good, they were making me uncomfortable.

If you are still with me, it's probably because, like me, you are self-conscious about your garden and, let's face it, how un- "Great Dixter" it is. I'm guessing you've been slapped around a bit by your failures too. Would you care to share a few of the questions you've been avoiding? Like, oh, I don't know:

Did you manage to plant a swath of *anything* out there? <*slap*>

Why is one's gaze led up the path right to the garbage bins? <*slapslap*>

That topiary looks like a lumpy duck! <*slap*>

Kniphofia?! <headlock> Explain yourself!

No, a Grievous Dixter doth your garden be. At very best a Subpar Dixter. And so is mine.

Fortunately, in the garden, as in life, there is no end to the amount of solace that can be wrested, kicking and screaming, from the greasy paws of *euphemism*. This magical slight of tongue makes the pain of your incompetence a little more bearable. It sugarcoats; it lets you down gently. It slaps on rose-tinted glasses that aren't *quite* the correct prescription, but are still an improvement because your own, actual rose is full of black spot and hasn't bloomed in years.

At a minimum, euphemism confuses things enough that we can lump our garden blues in with the general malaise of existence. Which can then be medicated or psychoanalyzed.

That it is a facile, reluctant solace, squeezed out under duress by a careful twisting of words does not matter to us insecure creatures who balk when compelled to describe our gardens. Because frankly, it's better than nothing. I don't have space for swaths, and you don't have time for topiary. Our Dixter dreams are untenable, so we'll take whatever consolation we can get.

In case you were worried, this use of cheap linguistic tricks to distract from horticultural shortcomings is a time-honored and wholly legitimate practice. Intentionally or not, gardeners have been gilding their floppy lilies with choice language for untold generations. After all, there is something unavoidably flimsy and false about the use of words to describe such an abstract expression as gardening. Whether we speak from shame, pride, or self-deception, no glib summary of a garden's summer's eve could hope to capture the soul and sacrifice that went into creating that moment. Its maddening failures, its flashes of brilliance, its chance harmonies and sudden quarrels—all are felt deeply, and no flapping of our clumsy tongue could sound the depths of these feelings. So much gets lost in translation because these are languages with little analog between them. In some regard, one can speak nothing *but* euphemism when asked to describe a garden.

That's my excuse anyway.

And while the device may not persuade others that your humble, mismatched smattering of plants is a masterpiece, a strategic deployment of euphemism can convince them temporarily that you yourself are mostly okay with the way your garden looks. Then, hopefully, while the wordy ruse still lingers, they will go away so you can cry into a bowl of chardonnay.

I never said it's a *healthy* way to deal with insecurities—it's just one tool in the toolbox, okay?

But before you poke your head out of the kitchen window to try some slippery lyrical countermeasures on your own garden, let's make sure you're doing it correctly. Improperly phrased, a euphemism can quickly morph into its dark cousin, Irony, and backfire on you. Then, instead of feeling a little better about the way things look out there, you could be nursing whiplash and glub-glubbing your vino ahead of schedule.

Take heart, that's why I'm here—to help twist the tongues of those who despair.

Well, that's *one* of the reasons why I'm here anyway.

You'll just have to trust me, while I can barely dog-paddle in the pool of garden design, I'm a pro at this. After a little practice together, you'll be well on your way to blissful bemusement. This is what I was meant to teach. I won't even charge you extra for the service! (Donations, however, are always appreciated.)

So let us *euphemize*, shall we?

First, go ahead and look around your garden. Soak it all in. What do you see?

Is it a mess? Mismatched? A bit random? Is there a lack of vision?

Of course not! It's *eclectic, free-spirited, wild*—a true *gardener's garden*. That's right. Ooh, this feels good, doesn't it?

Now, is it maybe immature? Amateur? Confusing? A bit jarring? Unfinished? No sirree it's not. It's *playful! Nuanced. Dramatic.* You know what—a *collector's garden* is what it is!

Who hasn't been on the wrong end of *that* euphemistic blunderbuss before, am I right? Yes, mine is resoundingly a *collector's* garden. It's a nice way of saying that I'm better at buying plants than I am at gardening. Thanks.

The goal in all of this, if you're feeling dirty and dishonest, is not to lie about a garden. We are not proclaiming the bad qualities to be good. The trick lies, rather, in expressing ambivalence with a smile. You are to be a fawning fanatic of the neutral, an enthusiastic champion of the self-evident.

This kind of functional fluency in euphemism will also allow you to comment on other gardeners' *handiwork* (see, there I go again) without the embarrassment to all parties of having offended their delicate pride. In person. Certainly your echoing flattery will start to ring a bit hollow later on, perhaps at night, in bed, when doubt so often rears its big misshapen head to snarl.

"Waitaminute!" it will roar. "What did he mean by 'a low-maintenance paradise'?! Is that even a good thing?" Not really. But you'll be long gone by then.

If you aren't yet sure whether you are cut out for this wizardry of words, don't worry! It often comes quite naturally for folks who would rather spend their time with poppies than with people. We have a way with words, and that way is to save them for when they are most needed.

Just remind yourself when commenting on your own garden or others': It's not the *plants'* fault they look bad together. They didn't magically self-assemble into a travesty. So even if you care little for propitiating the humans at hand, try to think of something at least superficially nice to say about the garden. Plants can't tell if you're being disingenuous, they just appreciate the lilting cadence of rote compliment.

"Would you look at that pieris! It's … *enormous*!"

"I don't think I've ever *seen* so many different heathers!"

"Wow! That rudbeckia is just, certainly … well, it's blooming its little head off, isn't it?"

Sorry, I may have tipped my hand there: I'm not the biggest fan of rudbeckia.

But I can't just *say* that now, can I? I can't blithely opine upon the glaring yellow-orange flowers that seem to shout over everything in the natural world, without considering their right to bloom or the possible reasons for their being planted in the first place. I don't have to like you, or even unduly care about you, in order to recognize the inherent validity of your horticultural voice.

Gardening, after all, is living poetry of the earth. And just as most poetry is awful to those who didn't write it, creating a garden, for us mortals, is not always an objectively triumphant endeavor in human artistry. It is, rather and simply, another of our species' endless forms of self-expression. The little leafy verses we plant in the soil whenever there's time and inspiration to do so, are just another way for us to see, outside, what we feel inside. They are how we externalize the turbulent gurgle of gentle madness we call creativity. Sometimes the result of these expressed feelings is a harmonious resonance that sings out between the world and us, and this is beauty, no matter what anyone else says. And sometimes ... well, sometimes you are feeling rudbeckia. And that's okay too.

Rudbeckia are ... *floriferous.*

The truth is, your poetry isn't awful, and neither is your garden. Not if you think of it as another *way* to speak rather than something to be spoken *of.* Whatever words you do conjure up in its defense are largely irrelevant, because the meaning of your garden is expressed in a different language anyway. Its greatness is implicit, its value unspoken. So shut up already.

And yes, my own garden may be more akin to a Great Sneeze than a Great Dixter, but here's what I'll tell you about my garden: It means a lot to me. More than could ever be expressed by whole breathtaking swaths in some stranger's famous garden.

Because I know that, even in their reticence, my hellebores speak of the coworkers who gave them to me on a birthday; the witch hazel, of all the growing years my wife and I have shared it; the blueberries, how they vanish into the purple-stained faces of my children each summer; and all those heathers … well, the heathers I got for free because a local nursery was throwing them out. Not everything is sentimental.

But if you do happen to ask someday about my garden, I suppose I'll tell you that it speaks for me in a way that my words can't. And if that means it doesn't always sing *Beauty!* in one choir-of-angels voice, then so be it. Neither do I. Still, if you're willing to stop talking for a moment and listen, I think you'll find its parts all have something to say.

And I'll bet your garden does too.

Recipes From My Garden

Zucchini Heap

Preparation Time: However long it takes to realize no one wants your zucchini.

Cook Time: No need to cook! Fresh zucchini make a wonderful heap all on their own!

1) Start with what seems like a modest amount of zucchini starts. Two or three should be good, right?

2) Wait a couple months.

3) Marvel at the satisfying, astounding health and vigor of your zucchini vines!

4) Begin harvest.

5) Bake a token batch of zucchini bread or something. Your options are limited; it's not really one of the better vegetables.

6) Arrange your now-numerous, ripe zucchini artistically on the windowsill to make your home look like a quaint, productive homestead. Go ahead and post on social media. Once the windowsill is full, such that you cannot possibly stack one more zucchini without hampering emergency egress from your home, move on to step seven.

7) It's pretty neat that you grew a vegetable, right? Won't other people think it's cool too? How special to give away some of your

beautiful, homegrown produce to friends, family, coworkers, neighbors, fellow bus riders, bike commuters waiting at traffic lights, stray dogs, and delivery truck drivers. Everyone likes zucchini, right?

8) No, they don't.

9) Really, stop it. No one's willing to say anything, but yeah, just stop with the zucchini.

10) Move your (now slowly rotting) kitchen pile of summer gourds outside somewhere. Just toss 'em anywhere. This is where the recipe is transformed from mundane to marvelous. Or, at least, from harvest to heap. Continue to add zucchini as the embarrassing bounty of their season unleashes

wave upon wave of blithe, bland gourds.

11) See how big your heap gets! Probably best not to post on social media at this point.

12) Don't grow zucchini next year.

Wild Forces

What happens when two of nature's most powerful forces collide? When the headlong drive for dominance meets terse civility with a crack of mighty thunder? Whose fangs will gleam the sharpest when teeth are flashed in cold smiles? Whose inferiority complex will ultimately prove superior? And can any victor emerge from the fray when the hot slash of shame draws blood equally in kind?

This week on "Wild Forces," it's Mother Nature at her most passive-aggressive. Join us for a bizarre encounter with that rarely filmed, oft-overlooked species: the Serious Gardener. We'll take a close-up look at these social but insecure creatures as they size each other up and attempt to establish hierarchy in their native habitat, the local garden center.

A battle to the death? Not even close. Will it come to blows? Unlikely. But might either of these proud animals fall, eviscerated, by the savage claws of horticultural one-upmanship?

Anything is possible.

Join us for a most-holds-barred grudge match between unnecessary rivals. Who grows the rarest plants? Who has visited the most gardens around the world? Who will be called out for mispronouncing botanical Latin? Who will be the last gardener standing, victorious, if a little bit silly? Stay tuned and find out … on Wild Forces!

<Bumbadum bum bumdadum baaaaa! Bum bumdadadum bumdadadum baa baaaa BAAAAA!>

We begin at the garden center. Spring. With the return of vernal warmth and longer days, gardeners congregate from miles around to slake the twin thirsts of their endeavor: a need for more plants, and the social validation to affirm the sanity of their pursuit. The scene is bustling, a veritable hive of goodwill, good cheer, and the exuberant promise of another year with dirt under one's nails. It is a place of lush vitality and peaceful enterprise.

Except … when it's not.

Plants Are Terrible People

For the Serious Gardener has much at stake here. In this complex hierarchy, he is of a different caste. Or so he likes to think. In reality, once he dons vest and clogs and starts puttering around, there is little observable difference in his behaviors—the tools he uses, the clothes he wears, the rituals he observes—to set him apart from all the so-called "casual" gardeners milling about on this bright April day. In fact, there is no hierarchy at all! It is all completely made up, fizzing about in his head. But he doesn't know that, or he has chosen to ignore it. And best not to tell him, as the bubbly delusion provides fascinating material for our program.

Observe, for example, the palpable disdain he shows for our camera crew as our producer James attempts to provoke a typical response from him.

(Do keep in mind, ours are experienced professionals. Under no circumstances should viewers attempt to interact with a Serious Gardener in the wild.)

Now, let's listen to James:

"Hey … hey there, buddy. I'm … I'm uh, looking for the *Hew-CHAIR-uhs*. Seen any of those? *Hew-CHAIR-uhs*?"

An innocent enough question. But baited with an irresistible morsel of botanical mispronunciation, which, to the Serious Gardener, screams 'amateur.'

Let's see how the gardener responds.

"Ugh. You mean *Heucheras*? No, I don't really bother with those anymore."

Disgust. Bile. Revulsion. His eyes tell the story of his disdain. His words too. If you were listening, his words do a fair job of telling the story. The combination is bristly and unpleasant. Pay attention as we goad him once more—for science, of course. Here's James:

"Hey, fella … hey. I was just over at Garden Depot and they've got those, uh, daisies you've got there for *way* cheaper."

This, invoking what is, to our specimen, an intolerable vulgarity of plant and place. Hackles up, he retaliates:

"Daisies? *DAISIES?!* You're joking, right? This is a rare *Olearia,* and no, they don't have them at *Garden Depot.* Even if they did, I would not buy them there. Because I don't *shop* at Garden Depot and neither should—wait, is … is that a camera?"

The crew has been spotted. Cover blown, they retreat to a safe distance, ducking behind a row of arborvitae.

Notice how the Serious Gardener violently resents any inference that his taste in plants—or retail establishments for that matter—might stoop to the ordinary. His pride does not allow him to like what he likes; he likes, rather, whatever confounds or contradicts the casual gardener. This is insecurity at its most—

"Hey, guys. I can still *hear* you, you know!"

The Serious Gardener has seen through our subterfuge. We must remain still and silent in order to avoid our encounter turning hostile.

"Yeah, those are *thujas* you're hiding behind, not a soundproof wall."

Ab-solutely silent ...

"Ugh. Whatever. I'll be over in Rare Plants if you feel like insulting me some more."

This could be the opportunity our crew has waited weeks for! The allure of rare and unusual plants is nearly irresistible to the Serious Gardener. The possibility of acquiring and planting something—of possessing *something—no other gardener has heard of, regardless of the plant's actual merit, sings like a siren, wafts on pheromones, and yanks our subject with a lasso. His self-control is utterly compromised. If we are to capture an encounter between two of these majestic, horticultural blockheads, it will most likely happen here, in the farthest, most isolated corner of the garden center, where astute nursery owners attempt to quarantine them and their snorting, prickly ilk. Let's follow along, quietly.*

"Hi again! Hey there, uh—I can still hear you. Are you aware that you're narrating out loud? Also, I can actually *see* you following along back there. You're not invisible or anything. Just thought you should know."

We must remain still ...

"Yeah, you just froze in place, but there's like six of you right there out in the open, with a camera. Plus, you know, your boom mike just knocked my hat off ..."

...

"<*sigh*> Oh well, at least they've got some new hepaticas today. Ooh, a double-flowered variety! I suppose I could make room for *one* more."

Our unsuspecting subject continues to—

"Oh, no I'm *totally* suspecting. I'm just ignoring you. Don't kid yourselves, guys."

—Continues to browse these choicest bites of horticultural decadence, conveniently forgetting that his garden at home is full. His potting shed is full. His deck and patio and kitchen windowsill and car seats are already chock full of teetering pots and plants. There is. No more. Room. Were he alone here, free of peer pressure, he might just be able to summon the will to refuse yet another addition to the overstuffed madness.

But our crew knows something he doesn't; he is about to be ambushed.

"Wait, what?!"

For what has our cameraman spotted but a second, *female, Serious Gardener, on rapid approach to the rare plants section. This could be the encounter we've been waiting for! What will our subject do when he is caught red-handed with a plant he cannot, by any measure of sanity, accommodate in his garden? Does he put it back, at the risk of appearing indecisive? Or does he hastily claim all the rest, assuring at least that no rival gardener will plant them if he himself cannot? The second gardener nears. Let's observe.*

"Hepaticas, huh? Which one you got there? Hmm, yeah, that's a decent one. Not especially vigorous, though. I've grown it for a few years now."

The new subject has come ROARING out to challenge our original subject. Just as he had begun to let his guard down and express cautious approval of a plant, she lashes out with barbed tongue at his soft, exposed underbelly. He is reeling.

"Yeah, no, I'm fine guys, but thanks."

"Um ... so what's with the film crew?"

"I have no idea. They seem ... mostly harmless? Obnoxious, though. Probably some internet thing. They think you're going to ... challenge me or something."

"Over ... *hepaticas*?"

"I guess. You can ask them, but they'll probably just freeze up and act like we can't see them."

Do not ... move ... a muscle.

"See?"

"Hmm. That's weird."

"Right? Anyway, you were saying you've grown this one?"

"Yeah, I fell in love with it on a garden tour over at Fencebroke Promontory and they happened to have a few for sale."

And just like that, the battle begins with the first name-drop. Our initial subject is burning with shame that his rival has drawn first blood using a casual mention of an obscure garden. Does she know who the head gardener is? Are they acquainted? He is left in a difficult position. He cannot come out and attack with these questions outright, but rather must call her bluff by implying that he himself might also be so privileged.

"I ... I'm not ashamed."

He is deeply *ashamed. Deeply. He is struggling to mount a defense.*

"Okay. Well anyway, yeah—I knew they were growing some at Fencebroke. This is the first time I've seen 'em at a nursery, though."

A feeble retaliatory strike. Mere repetition of the aforementioned garden, to lay some paltry claim to a shared familiarity. Let's see how the female responds.

"Uh ... oh—okay, I'm responding now, I guess. Well, honestly, I'd save your money. It's definitely a pretty little thing, but mine took a couple years to bloom and it's still about the same size as this one here."

A vicious attack! A snarling claim to dominance. 'Don't bother,' she says. Not only have I heard of this plant, I have already grown it and dismissed it as inferior. Save your money, so-called 'gardener'! Indeed!

"Look, guys, I don't know what you think is happening here. This is just the way that gardeners talk. She's already grown it and evaluated it, so now I don't need to waste space in my garden. We're not ... fighting, are we?"

"We are not. No. Ooh, they've got hardy Scheffleras!"

"Aren't they spectacular? I've got this one in a pot and it's *this* big!"

"No!"

"I kid you not."

A classic counter—invoking the Divine Specimen: "My skills as a gardener cannot be questioned," he is saying, "I have taken this rare plant and grown it to herculean perfection."

"Yeah, I didn't say that."

His Divine Specimen is of mythical stature, he boasts. Other, inferior gardeners would do well to bow out and cede the day to his, the greenest thumb.

"No, I'm saying it's a big plant."

"Yeah, I've got one too. It's also big."

She is not to be outdone! Her prowess is peerless! 'My plant is no less a colossus of health and vigor!' she bellows. 'I will devour you where you stand.'

"Okay, I've got to stop you there. 'I will devour you where you stand' does not exactly follow from what she said. Do you guys ever listen to yourselves?"

"Just ignore them. Hey, do you know anything about this one here?"

"Which, the eucomis?"

"No, I've given up on those. I mean this disporum, here."

The Serious Gardeners cannot maintain this level of fury for long. They have both sustained heavy injury and are close to exhaustion. Who will collapse first and yield to the other? Who will kiss the blade of their foe's Felcos? Which of these ... "Wild Forces" will prevail? We'll find out after a word from our sponsors!

"No. No way, I refuse to believe you nitwits have sponsors."

"I'm gonna do it. I'm gonna try the disporum."

"Oh yes, go for it! Let me know how it performs. Hey, are you going to the plant sale this weekend at the arboretum? I heard they're going to have—"

Mortal enemies, to the bitter end. There are no survivors when Serious Gardeners wage war. The herd is thinned but the species will go on. It must. For as long as new leaves unfurl there will be sunlight to—

"So, um, hey. It doesn't sound like these guys are going to stop anytime soon. We can just leave, right?"

"Yes. Yes, we can."

"Let's do that."

Missing!

Cultivator

Small, red, gas-powered mini-rototiller. Not so much "missing" as being held hostage by the yellow jackets whose nest I may have unwittingly plowed into. If someone wants to come retrieve it, that would be awesome. You don't even have to find it; it's right where I left it behind the house. I can see it out there right now, even as my eyelids are beginning to swell shut from the bee stings. The yellow jackets weren't in a mood to negotiate.

Wow, this is uncomfortable. Alarming even.

Hard to breathe.

You know what, forget the cultivator!

Call an Ambulance!

Kevin the Rutabaga

Kevin was a rutabaga. Not at first, mind you, it took some time. That is to say, he was always a *rutabaga*, but he wasn't always *Kevin*. It should surprise no one that most rutabagas go through life anonymous. Such would have been Kevin's fate as well, but for two important facts of his existence.

First, the garden where he sprouted: mine. If you've been paying attention, you know this is the plant equivalent of being born into one of those big, eccentric, dysfunctional families that everyone is scared of, but also kind of wishes they could join. Which is okay with me. You can join. All are welcome in this strange soil. Just watch out for toddlers with trowels. And plan on counseling somewhere down the road.

Second, this particular rutabaga demanded attention by rapidly growing larger than the others in his row. Much larger. Kevin—even before he was nominally so—came to resemble nothing so much as a great, bulging, purple football, lodged deep in the earth, having been punted from worlds away or great heights by some thunder-shod deity who couldn't convert on third down. And while such divine provenance may have raised certain theological questions, really it was no more absurd than some of our own professed origins. Gods, we have surely learned by now, are nothing if not capricious. Especially when it comes to recreation. However Kevin came to be, he came to be so with gusto. He was a freaky-big root growing in an already weird garden.

And he didn't stop. He kept right on growing, all through autumn, all through the winter. At a certain point, I had no choice but to take notice: a star was being born before my eyes. Which I mean in both the celebrity, paparazzi-hounded sense of the word, and presumably, if he kept up his unchecked expansion to the point of gravitational collapse, an actual, celestial star. Right there in my own vegetable garden. Before long, a dense cloud of social media followers and coalescing planets would begin swirling into orbit around him.

But it wasn't just his size that struck me. I had produced large veggies before—some corpulent tomatoes; a handful of well-endowed beans; that one feral zucchini that goes missing every year and shows up grotesque and engorged at season's end; even what I once thought were large rutabagas—but nothing like this. The thing of it was, Kevin wasn't just big, he was perfect.

At least the part that I could see was perfect, anyway. He flaunted a robust canopy of greens, smooth, strong shoulders jutting from the earth, unmarred skin rippling from creamy white right on past ultraviolet, and a poise and stature that placed his bearing somewhere between regal and military.

He was everything you could ask of a swollen, stew-bound winter root. Which, I get, isn't saying a lot, but if you're going to be a big fish in a small pond, why not be the 1200-pound tuna in a school of herring?

Probably because of sharks, come to think of it. Better to be the shark than the tuna.

Better still to stay away from marine-life metaphors in the first place.

But back to Kevin. Apart from his precocious physical growth, he began to grow on *me* too. At first, the personification of Kevin the Rutabaga was no more than a tacit acknowledgment of this change. *Hmm,* I'd think to myself, *that there rutabaga is an exceptional specimen. You're looking well today, rutabaga.* Or, *This is good. This fabulous rutabaga must mean that I am a good gardener. My vegetable garden will now have undeniable street cred. Respect from my family, peers, and society will surely follow. Thank you for this, fine rutabaga. I am in your debt.*

Yes, I realize there are any number psychiatric red flags in there. Welcome to the way I think.

As the weeks passed, and through whatever troubles presented themselves in the garden and beyond, I came to depend on the vitality of my bloated, earthbound 'baga-ball. Whether after a rough day of work, a rough day of life, or in the grip of agonizing masculine inadequacy wrought by too many chiseled abs and jawlines in the latest superhero movie, Kevin's healthy girth kept me positive. He came to embody everything that was stubbornly fine in life.

But, I realized one day, if he was going to properly embody anything at all, he ought to at least have a name. Right?

Right.

The christening itself came as little more than a joke. At least that's what I was hoping for. As I pulled aside the leaves to show my wife the progress of our garden one chilly afternoon, she gasped and said, "Wow! Holy rutabaga, what should we call it?"

To which I laughed a shrill, weird little laugh, and replied, without a pause, "KEVIN!"

To which *she* said nothing but got that funny look on her face like, was I all right?

Had I already decided on the name? Did it come to me on the spot? I can't say I recall, but either way, the damage was done. "Kevin" stuck, and what had previously been no more than an inanimate collection of brassicacious plant cells, was thereafter imbued with uppercase identity, transmuted in the reckless fires of anthropomorphism. Thus denoted Kevin was instantly hoisted above the nameless froth of meat and salad whose lives and deaths have gone uncapitalized throughout the eons. He would now stand exposed atop his new proper-noun pedestal, subject to the same scrutiny, elation, and misery endured by monikered mortals everywhere.

Because a funny thing happens when someone or something gains a name. When you realize the mailman is called "Anthony," and the checker at the grocery store has "Carole" on her name tag, and someone years ago painted *Matilda* on the back of that scrappy, rundown fishing boat you're thinking about buying, you can no longer pretend they mean nothing to you. These names take up space in your own life, in your mind, and whether or not you decide to care about them, they still symbolize an irrefutable presence and existence outside your own. The act of appellation shatters any solipsistic delusions still lingering from that one college philosophy course you took. It places you in the world relative to others—other entities who scatter names as they go, down the road through however many degrees of separation it takes to get from you to *Matilda*. It makes their fate significant to you, and yours to them, and changes destinies accordingly. A name is, in this way, a responsibility, a burden even. Unasked for, unwanted perhaps, but also unavoidable.

It's a lot to have placed on a rutabaga. I get that now.

In hindsight, I should not have named him. It made him more of a person, less the common turnip he deserved to be.

Plants Are Terrible People

In a world where even the best *people* can't help but to fall short of expectations, to disappoint and disappear, what chance did a plant have? Plants are terrible people.

But it's what we as humans do: We grow attached to anything that hangs around on this lurching bull of a world long enough to become familiar. We find it utterly endearing that something could coexist so well in time and space that it can hold on for dear life right alongside us. And oh the relief, when it can be found reliably and quickly, through blurry eyes or worried glances, right about where we left it. There is immense solace in this predictability, even if deep down we know it can't last. We'll take an illusion of permanence over one of isolation any day. This, the better to stave off the midnight madnesses that haunt our half-sleep. Like, what happens when the names we've come to know and love are suddenly for things remembered instead of things beheld? What do we do when the things are gone, and all we are left with are the names?

It's no wonder we might come to appreciate a steadfast rutabaga for being present when we do storm outside in our underwear at 2 a.m. on a sleepless winter night, shouting abandoned names to the stars and looking for the shape of anything familiar.

We all do that, right?

All I can say is, December is a chilly month for existential angst. But at least Kevin *was* still there, moonlit and magnificent in the garden, when I ran out in my skivvies to check. I was, for the moment, consoled. It may have led to more pain down the road, but to me he had earned his name.

The season crept along, and Kevin's growth finally slowed with the hard frost of winter. On especially frigid nights I worried, and it was more than a gardener's concern for the survival of his crops. Now there was a precise shape and name to my unease. More than once I snuck outside in the dark and hurriedly covered him with frost cloth and blankets. More than once my wife caught me sneaking back in. She would shake her head and I'd laugh like it was funny, but sometimes it's hard to tell.

Then, one warmish day, after long dark months of fretting about Kevin and trying and failing to explain to my kids who or what "Kevin" was, I knew the time had come. The air was fresh, Kevin had perked up in the dawning glimmer of spring, and the pragmatic side of me acknowledged that it wasn't going to get any easier.

Now, I know what you're thinking, but I felt no special sorrow that Kevin's time for harvest had come. What's a rutabaga for, after all, if not to yank from the ground at peak size and sweetness and roast into a delicious hereafter? This would be the fulfillment of everything Kevin was destined to be: dinner. I even envied the simplicity of his good fortune, the easy measure of his successful life. One could do worse, in my mind, than to provide hearty sustenance with the last of one's corporeal self.

But as I went to pull him gently from the earth, a wistful smile on my face, a faint, vernal melancholy in the air, I sensed immediately there was something wrong with Kevin, something heretofore hidden from view. There was no struggle commensurate with his presumed, deep anchorage, no jaws of stubborn life sunk into the earth he once seemed heaven-sent to swallow whole.

He just let go.

Kevin popped free from the soil with barely a tug, sending me sprawling over backward with the wasted inertia of my effort. My heart stopped. Or perhaps time simply slowed in that cheap trick the universe employs when exceptionally proud of a cruelty sprung in chaos from its loins. It is through moments like these we are meant to remember, in bruise-blue dreams ever after, that we were fools to believe a thing could last.

Okay, Universe. Duly noted.

Once I had been deemed sufficiently chastised by Time itself, and my heart reluctantly turned over to sputter on for however long it might, Kevin, or what was left of him, landed beside me, square in my disbelieving gaze.

Who among you, readers, has had the distinct privilege of eating good rutabaga? How many have tasted the winter sunshine delicately sequestered in this tough, unassuming taproot? Who has stood skeptically by while boiling pot or broiling flame worked a bit of magic on the chemistry of its humble flesh, turning cold, hard starch into sweet succulence? And who, once finally trying the stuff, has decided that, as a vegetable, this rutabaga thing is at least good enough to deserve a little more playing time in kitchen and garden?

Plants Are Terrible People

Well if you haven't yet, you should. Please, do not let what happened to poor Kevin taint your perception of untried root vegetables.

At first, after yanking him from the soil, I didn't quite understand what I was seeing. Granted, this is not an uncommon occurrence between The World and I, but this time, there was a moment where expectation and revelation so violently shook with dissonance that I could not reconcile the two into any sort of coherent narration of reality. Frankly, I felt like I might be sick. Looking back, I feel like I might still be.

Kevin's crown still looked lush and strong. Hence my confusion. From what had been the level of the soil and up, he was every bit the picture of health and vigor and stellar expansion I had come to rely on over the months. This was the part of him I recognized, the Kevin of which I'd grown fond, and proud to a degree perhaps unwise between a gardener and his crop. If I forced myself to only see this part—if I squinted just right and ran a finger along his smooth, familiar top—I could pretend he was fine. It was just like before. He'd be okay.

But he wasn't okay; he never would be again. The rest of Kevin, the 90 percent of the iceberg that had been his body below ground, was ravaged. What should have been an enormous cache of buried turnip treasure, was instead soft, rotten, and worm-riddled to such an extent that his apparent, above-ground vitality read as an unbearable non sequitur. Kevin was, somehow simultaneously, the picture of leafy, purple health, and a horrific subterranean snarl of ruined flesh.

I shuddered, aghast at the extent of his undermining, at the disgraceful collapse of this, my garden star, who was meant to blast through life and death in a supernova of winter stew. A silent gasp ran through the ether as betrayed minor planets and moons fell from Kevin's orbit in shock.

I wasn't ready or willing to see him like this—reduced suddenly and utterly to a mere mortal vegetable. Of course, he always *was* a vegetable. But now, eaten up and empty inside, the black spots and tunnels from voracious insects marking him well past the point of no return, he was never more clearly just fodder for the great, ever-grazing maw of the cosmos. His unspoken final words uttered that ours is a world that cares not for what we call rutabagas or whom we call Kevin, only that every named thing we cherish is too complicated and must be made simpler at all costs. To this end, there is an infinite toolbox of means, both clever and blunt: predation and happenstance, maggots and canker, gravity and plague. Whichever will come for us, by and by, is not a choice we get to make. And perhaps it doesn't matter so much, in the end, how we go or why, only that someone is out there, kneeling above us, whispering our name into the wind when we do.

The problem, for those of us left whispering, is that once a named thing is gone, it leaves behind a hole with the same name. The sudden void of its departure, which would have otherwise been filled quickly by the blithe march of life, fossilizes instead, hardening into and around a skeleton of shared time and common language, cementing for always the ragged shape of what was torn from the ground.

An obdurate bubble remains, bulging and looming into frame whenever thoughts are careless enough to drift. Every passing day bounces, booming, off its hollow shell. Memories rattle forever inside its reinforced walls, unable to break free into blessed oblivion. Its skin is rough, its surface frozen with the imagined agony of those unknowable final moments.

Dead-end questions are engraved there: Which worm wriggled through the heart; which infection spread too far; what did he feel and what did he know—irrelevant details for most garden vegetables' demise, but not for one with a name. Your run-of-the-mill, chewed up, blighted rutabaga might be tossed onto the compost heap with naught but a passing regret and a thought to what crop might take its place, but a rutabaga named Kevin cannot ever be supplanted. The next seed to drop there will do so in Kevin's spot. The next carrot or parsnip to take root can only be an impostor, scorned not for its own shortcomings or inadequacies, but for its audacity to be there when the one we knew by name cannot.

Sorry, *carrot*, you're no Kevin. Not even close.

Where does this leave the gardener, then? Plowing the plot under in rage? Quitting the garden altogether? Maybe just not naming the damned vegetables anymore. How many tragedies are worth bearing in pursuit of a nourishing stew? Perhaps it is time for the gardener to remember that he too has a name that takes up space in the world—planets of his own to keep spinning—and he'd do well to live accordingly.

In the meantime, since we all will be someday yanked from the soil, ready or not, healthy or rotten—and since the

146

cowardice of anonymity will do nothing to change this—why not learn a few more names while we can? As many vegetables as we can? As many plants; as many cats and dogs and chickens? As many strangers, brothers, neighbors, fishing boats, and fellow beings as we can—all the terrible, wonderful people passing through our lives we have this one fleeting chance to call by name.

Why not?

Recipes From My Garden

Fencebroke Promontory Pickles

Preparation Time: Best not to think about it.

Cook Time: Don't worry, you won't get that far

This recipe is the result of careful experimentation with, and modification of, many terrible pickle recipes. A labor of love, but it was worth it! I believe with this version I've managed to capture all the worst elements of the pickling process and combine them in one convenient recipe. If you're looking for a great way to spend most of a day with nothing to show for it, this one's for you! For all you parents out there, pickling is also a fantastic chance, if you needed another one, to lose your patience and blow up at your kids. What better way to pass down the time-honored rite of food preservation than brandishing a wide-mouth funnel at your offspring while threatening cruel and unusual punishment to the next troublemaker who throws a sterile canning-jar lid at her sister as you try not to drip sweat into the eternally boiling pot of water on the stove? Pretty much any other way.

1) Find the biggest danged pot you have and fill it with water. Put it on the stove and get it boiling.

2) Put your canning jars into the boiling water to sterilize them. Realize that even your biggest danged pot is not big enough to cover the jars.

Turn off the stove and go buy a bigger danged pot.

3) Fill the new pot with water and get *that* boiling. Sterilize your jars. Also the lids. But you didn't buy lids, did you? Guess what?

4) Turn off the stove, go back to the store and buy lids.

5) Boil the water again.

6) Prepare your cucumbers—slice them or whatever—it doesn't matter, you won't actually get around to using them, because:

7) You need way more ingredients than you thought you did for this crap. Pickling salt? Is that even a thing? Pickling spice? Heads of dill? *How* much vinegar?

8) Turn off the stove. Go back to the store and spend an hour trying to find this stuff. But you won't find it, not all of it. It's a lot of weird stuff. This is your first good chance to lose it if you've got kids, who will at some point have gone feral as you trek back and forth across the grocery store asking every employee whether dill *weed* or dill *seed* is an acceptable substitute for dill *heads* which no store in the county seems to have. Never mind, it doesn't matter. Fine, whatever, just buy something and get out of there before the unruly brood you're dragging along manages to convince fellow shoppers that you're a child abductor. "Trust me!" you'll holler and immediately regret.

"No kidnapper would put up with you turkeys!" Ooh, too far. Too far.

9) Buy the kids ice cream on the way home because you feel awful about what you said.

10) Take a deep breath when you get back into the kitchen. Be present. Remind yourself this whole canning thing is a worthwhile skill to learn and teach your children, that not so long ago, folks *had* to know this stuff in order to survive. You can do it. You can *do* it. Start that water boiling again.

11) Fetch down the enormous bottle of vinegar you bought a few years ago, when you *meant* to start canning. Wow, it's way up there. Banished to the top shelf. You can *just … about*

... *reach it*. Uh, maybe you should go get a step-stool or someth—

12) *<CRASH!!!>* Or, just knock it off the shelf and let it explode at your feet, unleashing a nostril-scorching tide of vinegar upon your godforsaken home. That works too. Have you ever wrung out vinegar from your socks? No? Well then, this recipe is a great chance to try something new!

13) Give up.

14) Add red or white wine liberally, to taste.

That's all there is to it! Once you've mastered the intermediate steps, if you get the urge to make pickles again, feel free to just skip ahead to step #14.

Red-Eye

I s there a doctor on board?!" A cry erupts from the back
of the plane. It's mid-flight, Dallas to London, and
everyone's asleep. Everyone except me. I never could
figure out how to flip the switch the way other folks do. Too
many ghosts waiting in the dark. Calling out for me, dragging
nails across the chalkboard of my dreams. Together, we're a
noisy bunch. I don't want to be "that guy" and turn my
monsters loose on a bunch of jet-lagged strangers chasing Z's
in the jet stream.

But some people aren't so polite.

"Please, anyone—a doctor! This man is in pain!"

So everyone's asleep except me and some lady hollering
about a doctor. The passengers begin to stir, sensing distress
through their earplugs, headphones, and Xanax dreams. I

sigh and rub my eyes, hoping someone else will step up and come to the rescue. For once. Just because I can't find sleep doesn't mean I'm not looking. Let some other stranger jump in to juggle the eggs of life when they'd rather be snoozing off a double scotch. I've made my omelets.

"*Ooooohhhh*—aah!" A long moan cracks into telltale shards of pain. Whispers start to bubble up and float down the aisle. There's concern amongst the passengers, but mostly for themselves. What's wrong? Am I next? Why now? What was the last thing I said to my daughter? What comes after? Why did I spend so much time watching reality cooking shows?

You can't blame them. Life seems frail when you're strapped inside a metal tube doing five hundred miles per hour thirty thousand feet up at two in the morning. Those are scary numbers piling up into a whole heap of mean math. But the joke's on them, the equation never changes. Life is frail wherever you are.

"*Ahh!* It hurts so much! I've never before experienced this much pain in my entire life!"

Jeez, fella, we get the point. All right, fine. That's how it's going to be? I crack my knuckles, flip up the little seat-back tray, and stand up with a yawn.

"A doctor, please! A nurse, a first responder, a vet even? Isn't there anyone who can help?!" The call for help is echoed up the plane. *A doctor ... a nurse ... a doctor!*

"I'm comin', I'm comin'," I mutter under my breath, working my way down the aisle.

"Who's that? Is that a doctor? A doctor!" I hear in my wake. They wish. Let 'em think what they want. I don't see anyone else stepping up.

Three rows from the back a man lies fetal in the aisle. Pale, sweating, getting older, but it shouldn't be his time yet. Shouldn't be, but you never know. Life doesn't care as much about time as people like to think.

Several worried passengers lean over from nearby seats. They look up at me and something like hope washes over their faces. More likely it's just relief that their own impotence won't spell the end for this poor guy tonight. They're biting their nails thinking, *oh good, someone else is here, maybe I can go back to sleep.*

Nah, people aren't all that bad. Most of them are just scared. They don't want some poor soul moaning his way across the Atlantic reminding them that life can up and quit at any time just for laughs.

But it can. I've seen it.

"Thank god! Are you a doctor?" the woman nearest the stricken man asks me with eyes as red as this damn flight. I ignore her.

"Hey mister! What's the problem?" I ask loudly of the guy in agony.

"I-I'm in agony!" He says. More passengers are crowding back around us.

"Give us some space, folks please. Thank you. Okay, yeah, I can see you're in pain—"

"Agony!"

"Right, agony. Sorry. Try to stay with me here, I'm going to ask a few more questions, see if I can't figure out what's wrong."

Is he a doctor? I don't know, I think so. Whispers behind me.

"O-okay," the man says weakly.

"That's good. All right, where does it hurt?"

"Oooh, everywhere! I've never before experienced this much pain in—"

"In your entire life. Yes, I've heard. It sounds like something systemic. Tell me, have you been watered recently?"

…

"Have I … wait, *what?*"

"Water. You. Have you. Been watered. Recently?" I always start with the basics. "And how often are you usually watered?" The other passengers have stopped whispering. It's gone dead quiet but for the muffled roar of jet engines hurtling us all through the air. Which isn't really all that quiet, but at least I can hear myself think.

"I … don't know?" the man offers, confused. It was a simple question.

"Okay, forget the water for now. How about pests? Have you noticed any unwanted insects on your body recently? Are you prone to blights or mildews?"

"I … I guess I've felt a little weak, but—"

"*Waitwaitwait!*" somebody pipes up from behind me. Here it comes. "What … what kind of doctor are you, exactly?"

The world wants labels. You're nothing to them without a title, a prefix.

"I'm ... a horticulturist," I sigh, dreading the conversation to come. "I do not have a 'medical' degree." My finger quotes slash the air with disdain. Or maybe it's just fatigue. "May I continue, or does someone else want to ... no? Didn't think so. Okay, now sir, have you been feeling soggy as well as weak lately? It's very important that—"

"Hold on, you're a horticulturalist? Like what, a landscaper?"

"No, no—a horticulturalist. That means he grows *weed*. You know, mari-*juana*."

"HOR-TI-CULTUR-IST*,"* I correct them. "And I do not grow weed. I work with—"

"Yeah, come on," a new voice chimes in from somewhere. The plane is cramped, so I can't see any of these people. "Show some respect, this man is a farmer. Where do you think our food comes from, after all? I'll tell you: it comes from this guy's cornfields and cows and—"

"Please!" I interrupt. "This poor man may be damping off even as we speak! I must finish my diagnosis. Also, I don't grow corn and I don't have cows. You're thinking of—"

"Of course, you moron, dairy's a dying business." This in the cocky, high-pitched voice of someone I don't want to get started. The type with a six-shooter of speeches and an itchy tongue, quick on the draw. "He probably grows almonds." Yep, here we go. "Sucking the last of the water out of an already-drought-ridden Southwest so that rich snobs can have almond milk in their lattes. I bet—"

"PLANTS! OKAY? PLANTS!" I bark at the imbecile lot of them. "I work with plants. Like, for your garden? Now can I please get back to—"

"W-wait. What? You're a plant doctor?" The man on the floor speaks up, seeming to forget his pain for the moment.

"I'm, no … I actually studied botany, but I'm not—"

"But that dude is, like, not a plant!" some smart-ass shouts from farther up the plane.

"Yes, okay … I can see that." This is what I get for trying to help. "He's a man. I know. But … it's all just life, right? Plants, animals—we all use the same DNA. We all get sick eventually. I've rescued plants in worse shape than this guy. And I've lost some too. That's the way—"

"What?!"

"You've *lost* some? What does that mean, you've lost—"

160

"Plants or people?"

"Pfft! He's not a doctor—"

"Wait, almond milk is bad now?"

"Hey, I've got this rhododendron at home that's got these holes in the leaves—"

"For the love of god, is there a *people* doctor on board?"

"He's not even a *plant* doctor. My friend Sharon is a Master Gardener and she says … "

The yammering continues. I'm used to it, but that doesn't mean I like it. No one understands what it is I do. It's not that complicated. What do any of us do? We live, we breathe, we grow and make babies and eat half-price pizza on Thursdays while we can. If that seems to be going all right, well, then we reach out and grab onto a few other living things within arm's reach. We do what we can to keep *them* alive and breathing for as long as we can. All I'm trying to tell these people is that I keep things alive, every day, as part of my job. So maybe, just maybe, I can help this guy.

But I also know that plants and people are both made of fickle, fragile stuff that lets you know when it's had enough. And then it doesn't matter how tight you're holding on. Loving a bunch of brittle bones and stems means someday letting go of the pieces. Is it the end for this fella? I don't know, but I'm sure as hell going to hold on until we know for sure. Because no one else is.

"Please!" I make one last appeal to reason. "Would someone *please* go get my carry-on bag? There's a little shampoo bottle of copper fungicide in there that I always bring with me—"

"No, no—you know what?" The man in the aisle sits up, gaining a remarkable amount of strength in such a short time. "I … I think I'm feeling a little better. No need for … fungicide. I'll be okay."

Silence for a moment. Eventually, a smattering of confused, half-hearted applause flits around the cabin. Hallelujah, I guess. Everyone go back to sleep. I don't know if it was divine intervention, or the guy was faking the whole episode, or if he just mistook a bit of turbulence for the weightless eternity that stretches out before our last fall. Either way he'll get another chance to talk to his daughter. Another slice of pepperoni if he makes it to Thursday.

Just for good measure I grab one of those little airline-issue bottles of drinking water and empty it over the guy's head, so he doesn't dry out. Then I turn around and head back to my seat.

"*It's a miracle!*"

"*Is it?*"

"*Wait … what happened? I couldn't see anything from back here!*"

"*I wonder what my Master Gardener friend Sharon could do to help with these darn headaches I've been having—*"

"*I'm telling you, it's weed! Gotta be. Did you know the medicinal properties of marijuana have been known since—*"

"*Anyway, this rhododendron—at first I thought it was weevils, but—*"

"*So, was he a doctor or not?*"

Let them wonder. If you ask me, the only mystery to life is when it starts to make sense.

"*Pssst—hey, man! Dr. Horticulture—you got any more of that weed, man?*"

"*<Sigh>*"

Missing!

Pair of Knees

Heavily used. They left in a huff after a long weekend (and career) spent weeding.

They've given out on me before, and have been quick to complain in recent years, but this is the first time they've just left.

Now I can't find them anywhere. I even tried luring them back with a pair of fancy new kneepads.

They're not falling for that trick.

Please return promptly if found. I've been wiggling around the house like a bird-pecked worm for the last few days.

Reward:

One pair of fancy new kneepads. I never wear these things anyway.

Sweeping Up (Thoughts from the Dustpan)

Oh, whoops—hi there! Hey, sorry. Boy, that's embarrassing, you caught me leaning on my broom. Guess I thought everyone had gone home. No, no—it's all right, feel free to stick around if you don't mind me rambling on a bit. I was just doing some sweeping up. And thinking. One often leads to the other I've found. Keep your hands busy and your mind free; that's what I always say.

Well, I've never actually *said* it, but the sentiment is there. Somewhere. All part of an elusive, unspoken philosophy which occasionally flits across the outskirts of my mind. Like a fly, buzzing around. Usually while sweeping, come to think of it. Something about the job makes one an easy target for flies and philosophy. Either will keep you swatting and flailing through the day as good as the other. Leaning on the broom? Not so much. But hey, I'm tired. It's been a long book. Give me a break.

<Sigh> The truth is, I've spent an awful lot of time sweeping in my life. There's no way around it. Every job I've ever had has put a broom in my hand, including, and—who am I kidding—*especially* gardening. So many brooms in my hand. But what are you gonna do? It *is* a dirty job. Quite possibly, it's the *original* dirty job. Gardening is just the end result of our ancestors playing in the dirt long enough for carrots to happen. However much later brooms showed up on the scene, one must imagine they were embraced wholeheartedly by our gardener forebears, who could presumably recognize a match made in heaven when they saw one.

But you all should know this love story better than most. Yes, *you.* Don't think I haven't seen you walking around the flower and garden show with that fancy new outdoor broom you just bought, so excited to bring it home and try it out.

Let me repeat that: Excited. To try out a broom.

But no, hey, I get it. Trust me, I do. If you're going to spend a good portion of your waking (or sleeping) hours sweeping, you may as well try to find some joy in it, right?

…

Sleep sweeping? No, yeah, it's a thing.

…

Oh come on, I can't be the only broom-wielding sleepwalker out there, can I? It's a big world, there must be others—

Okay fine, it's just me. Let's not make a big deal out of it. It's mostly harmless anyway. I mean … well, there was the *one* time I woke up sweeping that abandoned bowling alley outside of town, but now, my family just barricades the doors at night, and we wake up with clean floors. It's fine.

Still, my nocturnal housekeeping idiosyncrasies would at least seem to vouch for the assertion that I've spent a good chunk of time swishing at dust bunnies in my life. (Also, *real* bunnies—those things are worse than vermin in some gardens—but we'll save them for another time.)

Yes, more so than spades, more so than shears, loppers, and forks, I feel I've gone through garden and life armed with this trusty, stiff-bristled sword. Apart we are mere tools, but together we are unstoppable. Across this land we've traveled, fighting leaf and litter in the name of clean walkways everywhere.

Which, I'll admit, sounds cooler than it is.

Or does it?

Perhaps not. I suspect there's not much that can be done, public relations-wise, to boost perception of the broomish arts at this point in history. Too long have they been relegated to their namesake closets in the eyes of society. Disrespected. Denigrated. Overlooked. Next to the rubber gloves and window cleaner. Along with us dutiful custodians who bustle and broom through the background of life, rarely if ever breaking into song and dance to endear ourselves to audiences the way our culture's rich, if deceptive, tradition of musicals might lead them to expect. By our unfinished work, you'd surely notice if we were gone, but not that *we* were gone. For we are everywhere, yet we are nowhere. We are everyone and no one.

Again, that *kinda* sounds cool, but it's not. I mean only to say that people don't care who holds the broom; so long as the mess goes away.

And that's okay. I didn't start sweeping because it was cool, or to make friends. In fact, I think it's safe to say I've never done anything to intentionally advance either of those causes. Hmm. No, I started sweeping because it needed to be done. I stepped up. No one else was doing it, or no one else was doing it correctly, so I pulled that sword from the stone and crowned myself the King of Clean, Vanquisher of All Things Spilled and Fallen.

I know, I know, that one doesn't even *sound* cool. I tried. It's just dumb. King of Clean—sure, it was cute and quirky at first, when I started wearing an actual crown, but, well, it got sad in a hurry. For anyone who might be searching, let me save you some time: it's nearly impossible to find a good quality, but affordable crown that doesn't immediately declare you an impostor.

Also, it turns out that All Things Spilled and Fallen are not so readily vanquished as they are, at best, stymied for a moment or two until Something Else is Spilled or Fallen. It is a Sisyphean task befitting no sane or proper King. Not that I had any legitimate claim to such a throne, but even delusional monarchies ought to be subject to some sort of internal logic.

So now I just sweep. And think. And yes, sometimes, I lean. No crown. Not even a scepter. Just me and the broom. And I'll tell you what's funny: I think I've learned more—or at least convinced myself of more—about the world while sweeping than during any other stage of my education or career. Perhaps that says something unflattering about my curriculum vitae, but there it is.

While it may not be as glamorous as planting crocuses or clipping hedges, there is a pensive dignity to sweeping. In pushing around the little piles, in effecting these humble, tidy strokes, one borrows a kind of thoughtful, pendulous momentum from the rhythm of life. Swaying to a fugue of chaos and order played out at the head of a broom, one catches fleeting truths: intricate melodies of organization and structure, with thundering counterpoints of gravity and decay. Back and forth.

One sees magnificently improbable towers of life, no sooner assembled from scratch into butterflies and maples, than blown to bits on the deep breath of time, a litter of fallen wings and leaves. Back and forth.

One sees ancient trees sprouting from seed; loves-of-lives burgeoning from strangers' lingering glances; aphids appearing from thin air—every uncanny genesis of complexity by which we live and measure life, all in time reverting to humus and soil for the next seeds to sprout anew. Back and forth.

As we sweep, each stunning impression of garden and stone, of flesh and bone, crumbles to a quintillion jigsaw pieces underfoot, only to spontaneously reassemble elsewhere, forming new puzzles with new pictures. It is a cycle at once comforting for its persistence and reviled for its failure to ever reproduce the same picture that just crumbled before our eyes.

You can see why most folks are hesitant to grab a broom. They would prefer to keep their minds busy and hands free than have to confront the existential bogeymen hiding in the dark, dusty corners of unswept floors. Can't say I blame them.

To the sweeper, though, such thoughts can be unavoidable. During the fraught aftermaths of life's messier moments, when no one else seems eager to pick up the pieces, our brooms whisper secrets as they traverse the rubbish and ruin. Once you are charged with cleaning up, you cannot help but to listen for the next shatter or fall. When breath comes with a rasp of bristles you can no longer deny that all things will collapse to the ground, eventually. And the cursed broom won't leave off there. *For even our own bodies*, it mutters, *someday, will be as clods of dirt scooched into the dustpan.*

Thanks for that, broom.

Of course, all these lurking janitorial epiphanies presuppose one has learned to sweep properly in the first place; that one speaks the language. And not many do. We are misled to believe that we'll simply know what to do when things start falling off the shelves and raining down around us. How hard can it be to push a broom, after all? How hard to make the shards and broken branches go away?

Harder than you think. But, since they don't teach broom skills in public schools anymore, and since the honorable, manual removal of fallen debris is rapidly becoming obsolete with the rest of our sacred and mundane connections to life's untidiness, you'll just have to go grab a handle and learn it the hard way.

Like I did. Lest you think it happened overnight, or that your trusty narrator is some natural, broomstick prodigy: I wasn't born with this easy stroke. I couldn't always banish dinge and detritus with a flick of the wrist as I do now. But, after years of flailing at floors in the wake of seasons and storms, I came to know the broom: its function, its purpose, its admirable, diametric stance against the sullying forces of time.

Still more years later and I *became* the broom. It and the dustpan grew as appendages of my very being. I was both the sweeper and the swept. I lived in the cracks and cackled in the gaps between hard, uncaring earth and the plastic bristles of humanity. Within this interface, I and all the cosmos were born and bloomed and rotted. I laughed at the impermanence, lamented the intransigence, and raged at the unfairness of it all. I saw men falling as leaves, leaves flying like birds, and birds sinking like stones into bottomless dark oceans of pavement.

Then I took a break from sweeping for a while. It was getting weird.

The point is, while I would never dare claim *mastery* of any gardening subject or skill, despite having plied the trade for well over a decade, I wouldn't hesitate to don whatever combination of epaulets, belts, hats, and ceremonial sashes one earns along the way to indicate ultimate command of broom and pile. (And don't tell me there's not a hat. There had better be a hat.)

With all that being said, I'm not one to boast. Which means you can rest assured any lofty self-evaluation in this matter is strictly for rhetorical purposes and not for glory. It is no matter to me which honorifics ought to accompany the stature of a tenured sweeper. You *may*, if you *choose*, refer to me as "Sweepy Sensei," or "The Broomed One," but by no means are you required to address me thus. It is, however, always appreciated.

And if you remain skeptical of my claims, then please challenge me here and now. I dare you to search for any chink in my armor, even the smallest of gaps in my diverse sweeping portfolio. Question my right to draw broad, *sweeping* conclusions with my broom. Come now, hold my hard-swept wisdom up to the light.

Go on: you name it and I've surely swept it.

But you probably won't play along, so allow me.

Where to start? Well, I've swept walkways, of course. Driveways. Pretty much all the "-ways". All the usual avenues and elevations. Sidewalks, stairs, ramps, and paths. Stepping stones. Decks and patios; chairs, benches, and chaise longues. A spectrum of tables from bistro to picnic. Outdoor rugs and AstroTurf. Innumerable surfaces to stride across, to sit and set upon. Be they upholstered or bare; tiled, bricked or paved. Be they soft, hard, or whatever adjective one might wave at the tactile enigma that is AstroTurf.

I've swept storm drains and gutters. Downspouts. Roofs and sills, window wells and soffits. Handrails and mailboxes and more semi-obscene garden gnomes than I care to recall. Potting sheds: he-sheds and she-sheds. Birdbaths. Plenty of nooks and a fair few crannies. Every incidental ledge, ornament, or protrusion bold enough to collect the settling silt of the world. I've swept them all; relieved them their burden of filth.

Tenderly has my broom brushed mulch from soft leather car seats, pellets of fertilizer from mansion floors, and crumbs of potting soil from exquisitely appointed houseboats. Together we have danced on balconies above sunset cliffs and verandas with more square footage than most reasonable homes. Priceless art, I've swept it. Statues of commissioned marble and copper; twisted, sculptural abstractions of form and finance—lo, have I unsullied the gilding and safeguarded property values with naught but a flourish and stroke!

But let us not forget the dark side of the broom. For I have swept what others won't. Spiderwebs from doorways; ants from their cracks; piles of dead wasps; excrement and effluvia; blood and bile. I've escorted poisoned rodents and brittle-stiff birds into the dustpan. Dead creatures and their maggot spawn—into the trash. I've swept up rats' nests and birds' nests and hornets' nests. Their homes, really. I've swept away any evidence of life having lived, and life having died, that others might be spared any connection between the two.

But connected they are, life and death. And equally messy. Yes, I've gone through after both, dragged a broom into the stillness that lingers afterward. After concerts and soirees, casual meetings and graduation buffets. The beheaded piñatas and glitter. The hors d'oeuvres on the ground. I've swept after weekend projects and month-long garden installs; after big sales and bigger storms; from finishing touches to fallen limbs. I've swept after house parties gone wrong, and bachelor parties done right. After "Surprise!" and "Kiss the bride," and "*Many Mooooore.*" And more glitter. More shiny, tiny fragments of something to be remembered. I've swept up confetti and rice; crumpled coffee cups; the somber dust of too many strangers' feet. Popped balloons and fallen clouds of cottonwood. Still more glitter. Maybe the same glitter. I've swept after last call … and lights out … and last words.

And the morning after.

And the morning after that.

I've swept to get through. Through the anger and grief, the excitement and exhaustion. Through quotidian joys and tectonic despair to the other side, if it's out there. Through the agony and apathy to some clean corner of peace.

I've swept in remembrance, and to forget, and to hide the evidence of a thousand clumsy lapses of heart and hand. After sowing and solstice, harvest and husk. After birthday and wedding and funeral, pushing my broom down the whole goddamned, beautiful gauntlet of the world as it shreds a man to glitter.

In some cases, I've swept because, sometimes, what else can you do?

And you know what? After all that sweeping? Well, I'll be darned if it all feels any cleaner than when I started.

But maybe that was never the point.

Nature abhors a vacuum, after all. And however many cleaning robots we buy, last I checked humans were still part of nature. We could sweep furiously for the rest of our days and still leave behind a mess because we can't help but to fall to pieces with everything else. All beings join the clutter in turn. Each beloved stack of matter, each bundle of stolen energy is returned in due time to fill the abhorrent void.

The universe gets what it wants, that diva.

So, I could get angry about it. I have before. I could gnash my teeth and rage that all my fervent sweeping has paid not one penny of interest on the debt we owe the cosmos for the thermodynamic temerity of our existence. But, 1) I don't precisely know *how* to gnash my teeth and, 2) What would be the point, shaking my broom at the heavens like a batty old curmudgeon? What's next, should I curse the shattered rose for its fallen petals, or bemoan the tree whose leaves shook loose before their season? How could I, when in life one took my breath away, and the other returned it, sweeter, to the world? There isn't enough ire in the well of mankind to anoint all the things that fail to last.

In sweeping up, our actions are no more permanent than they ever are. No sooner does a sigh of completion escape our lips than nature howls in on fresh eddies of mess. But we are, as sweepers, uniquely positioned to observe a great many precious befores and hallowed afters. We are afforded the privilege of both witness and memory; of seeing life whole, and in pieces; as it teeters triumphantly, and then falls; as it is, and as we all someday will be.

So, if you must know, I don't sweep to clean. As silly as that sounds for someone who can't even somnambulate without dancing the broom ballet. Rather, I sweep to brush clear the Earth, momentarily, for however brief a gasp, that those who come through after might distinguish their own fallen from the clutter of twigs and souls that would otherwise bury the world in a thick mulch of perdition and grief.

I sweep because, whatever futility or unfairness piles up at the broom end of life, someone ought to come through after and acknowledge what we were before we fell.

I sweep because the balance of life is not found in the sum total of its pieces, or even in the privilege of knowing the whole, but rather in the difference between the two.

The Broomed One sweeps so that he might know the difference.

At least, that's what he was trying to do before *someone* interrupted him.

Now, good lord, that's all I have to say about sweeping! So, if you'd be so kind as to get out of here already—I reckon I've been leaning on my broom long enough. Time to get back to it.

Recipes From My Garden

Remember

Preparation Time: 0-1 lifetime

Cook Time: However long you have

1) Step outside. Into your yard or neighborhood; a nearby park or community plot; onto your patio, balcony, or rooftop; through the woods, across the sand, along the side of the road. Step outside into the open air of the garden. Breathe deeply.

2) Remember.

3) Remember, if you can, the first time you planted a seed. In a childhood classroom, perhaps? Peas

or beans? A few pots of herbs in the kitchen window of your first apartment? Or maybe squatting in the early spring sunshine over cool dirt, trying hard not to spill the little handful of lettuce seeds with which you'd been entrusted? Poke a hole, drop the seed, cover it with soil, water, and … wait.

4) Remember checking daily, still skeptical of this magic act you'd been asked to believe in.

5) Remember that astonishing morning when the magic became real! Those first leaves sprouting through the soil.

6) Remember, try to remember, your heart sprouting at the same time! With a new delight, a new love.

7) Remember (as if you could forget) the ones who taught you, who passed on this gift before passing on.

8) Remember why *you* became a magician. A gardener. Remember and then pass it along.

9) Remember now, don't forget! Because someday the memories will be all we have, and then all we are. But the *garden* ... the garden will always be there. Right outside.

10) So go ahead. Step outside.

Luke Ruggenberg

The End

Luke Ruggenberg

Acknowledgments

A very heartfelt thanks to my brother, Jesse Ruggenberg and mother, Jodi Ruggenberg, without whose honest and meticulous editing this book would have been something of a mess; also to my talented and wonderful wife, Veronica Ruggenberg for her work on the cover and for her love and support in this project and life beyond. I have no commensurate way to repay these wonderful people's generosity of time; all I can offer is my gratitude.

Thanks to my children, Daisy and Rowan, for their levity, spark, and patience when Daddy's gaze went blank from staring at the page too long. To my entire family, each of whom provided encouragement and support as I set about creating these weird little books: my thanks and my love; I would not and could not have done any of this without you all.

Thank you to the entire crew at Ravenna Gardens, the best little garden center in the world. A man could not ask for better coworkers or a more inspiring place to work. Being surrounded by beautiful plants and lovely, caring people has helped keep me going through a difficult time.

Finally, a great and eternally echoing thanks bellowed into the depths of our universe, for the privilege of having known my late brother, Griffin. It was he who sparked in me the very love for plants that brought me to these pages.

Brother, I miss you. This one is for you.

About The Author

Luke Ruggenberg has worked as a gardener and horticulturist for quite some time now. It makes his back hurt just thinking about it. He has been a writer for a long time too, but that doesn't hurt his back as much. His previous book is *Twenty Reasons Not To Garden (And Why I Ignore Them All)* and he maintains a blog at *Fencebroke Promontory Gardens.*

Luke lives in the Pacific Northwest with his wife and two children, who are extraordinary and seem to tolerate him most of the time. This fact makes him want to high-five random passers-by.

For a virtual high-five, feel free to follow Luke on:

Twitter: @LukeRuggenberg

Instagram: lukeruggenberg

Or stop by lukeruggenberg.com

Made in the USA
Monee, IL
16 December 2020

53857863R00121